CW00537552

Magento 1.3: PHP Developer's Guide

Design, develop, and deploy feature-rich Magento online stores with PHP coding

Jamie Huskisson

PUBLISHING

BIRMINGHAM - MUMBAI

Magento 1.3: PHP Developer's Guide

Copyright © 2010 Packt Publishing

All rights reserved. No part of this book may be reproduced, stored in a retrieval system, or transmitted in any form or by any means, without the prior written permission of the publisher, except in the case of brief quotations embedded in critical articles or reviews.

Every effort has been made in the preparation of this book to ensure the accuracy of the information presented. However, the information contained in this book is sold without warranty, either express or implied. Neither the author, nor Packt Publishing, and its dealers and distributors will be held liable for any damages caused or alleged to be caused directly or indirectly by this book.

Packt Publishing has endeavored to provide trademark information about all of the companies and products mentioned in this book by the appropriate use of capitals. However, Packt Publishing cannot guarantee the accuracy of this information.

First published: January 2010

Production Reference: 1150110

Published by Packt Publishing Ltd.
32 Lincoln Road
Olton
Birmingham, B27 6PA, UK.

ISBN 978-1-847197-42-9

www.packtpub.com

Cover Image by Vinayak Chittar (vinayak.chittar@gmail.com)

Credits

Author
Jamie Huskisson

Reviewers
Jose Argudo
Erik Hansen

Acquisition Editor
Douglas Paterson

Development Editor
Swapna Verlekar

Technical Editor
Aditya Belpathak

Indexer
Hemangini Bari

Editorial Team Leader
Abhijeet Deobhakta

Project Team Leader
Lata Basantani

Project Coordinator
Joel Goveya

Proofreader
Sandra Hopper

Production Coordinator
Adline Swetha Jesuthas

Cover Work
Adline Swetha Jesuthas

About the Author

Jamie Huskisson, a passionate 23-year-old freelance developer from Nottingham, has been working with Magento for the past two years since the very early BETA versions. His development client list features names such as NHS, Volkswagen, and Nike with his day-to-day work life spent building everything from web applications to e-commerce stores and small business sites. He also trains groups of developers, and provides consulting on adopting open source technologies over closed systems for clients when required.

Jamie also writes and maintains a popular online blog at http://www.jhuskisson.com/ where he gives advice on various aspects of the web, including freelancing, Magento, Wordpress, PHP, and running your own business.

I'd like to thank my girlfriend Vicky for putting up with my late nights working on the book. I'd also like to thank my family and especially my mother, for raising me to believe that I can achieve anything I put my mind to.

To everyone that reads this, enjoy your time developing what you read in and out of this book. I look forward to hearing from any of you that develop sites or modules based on what you read between these covers.

About the Reviewers

Jose Argudo is a web developer from Valencia, Spain. After finishing his studies, he started working for a web design company. After six years of working for that company, and others, he decided to start working as a freelancer.

Now, he thinks it's the best decision that he has ever taken, a decision that lets him work with the tools that he likes, such as Joomla!, CodeIgniter, CakePHP, jQuery, and other known open source technologies.

In the last few months, he has reviewed books for Packt Publications such as Magento 1.3 Theme Design, Magento: Beginner's Guide, Joomla! 1.5 SEO, Joomla! with Flash, and Symfony 1.3 Web Application Development, along with Magento 1.3: PHP Developer's Guide.

If that weren't enough, he authored CodeIgniter 1.7 for Packt Publications, a book that he put a lot of effort into.

To my brother, I wish him the best.

Erik Hansen is an entrepreneurial techie with a bent for business. He's the co-founder and CTO of Classy Llama Studios, an e-commerce-centric company that he helped start in 2007. He leads a team of developers in providing creative solutions for Classy Llama's clients.

Hansen's interest in technology is hard-wired in his brain. He started out building basic circuit boards in his basement as a child, and after being involved in a number of startups right out of high school, he focused his efforts to become an expert in Magento e-commerce development.

When he's not staying up until the wee hours of the morning programming (on his MacBook Pro, of course), Hansen enjoys spending time with family and friends, reading, playing sports, and listening to music.

I would like to thank Kurt Theobald, Timothy Rhodes, Matt Johnson, and the rest of the Classy Llama team for investing their time in my personal development.

Table of Contents

Preface

Magento 1.3: PHP Developer's Guide will guide you through development with Magento, an open source e-commerce platform. Exploring commonly approached areas of Magento development, Magento 1.3: PHP Developer's Guide provides you with all the information you'll need to get a very solid understanding of developing with Magento.

What this book covers

Chapter 1, *Magento 3.1: PHP Developer's Guide* shows you what this book will cover entirely in detail for you to read through.

Chapter 2, *Installing/Upgrading Magento and Preparing for Development* will prepare you for development with Magento as well as showing you how to install and upgrade Magento using a variety of different methods.

Chapter 3, *Magento's Architecture* introduces you to Magento's architecture, the Zend framework, and how the system works from a development point of view.

Chapter 4, *Shipping Modules in Magento* shows you how to put together shipping modules in Magento to handle shipping calculation and information.

Chapter 5, *Building a Payment Module for Magento* guides you in putting together payment methods in Magento and building connecting modules between Magento and the payment gateway of your choice.

Chapter 6, *Building a Basic Featured Products Module* walks you through building a featured product module into your web site so that you can show featured products in your Magento categories.

Chapter 7, *Fully-Featured Module for Magento with Admin Panel* shows you how to put together a fully featured module in Magento as well as giving it a full backend to manage data with. You'll also learn how to use the module creator to quickly deploy module skeletons to use yourself in the future.

Chapter 8, *Integration of Third-Party CMS* will show you how to integrate Wordpress with your Magento installation. It will also show you the other options available should you use any other content management systems.

Chapter 9, *Magento's Core API* guides you through the Magento Core API and how to utilize it with scripts of your own to interface with Magento's data.

Chapter 10, *Importing and Exporting Data* shows you how to work with import and export data profiles in Magento to work with basic order, product, and customer data.

Appendix, *Resources for Further Learning*, contains additional resources for further learning. Its not a part of this book and it can be downloaded from Packt's website `//www.packtpub.com/files/7429-Appendix-Resouces-for-Further-Learning.pdf`.

What you need for this book

You will need an installation of Magento, either on your local machine or on a remote server, your favorite code editor, and permissions to manipulate files.

Who this book is for

If you are a PHP developer who wants to understand the architecture of Magento, learn how to extend the system with PHP code, add new features, and integrate Magento with a third-party CMS, this book is for you.

You are expected to be a confident PHP 5 developer. No experience of Magento development is expected, although you should be familiar with the operation of Magento. No experience of the Zend framework is expected.

Conventions

In this book, you will find a number of styles of text that distinguish between different kinds of information. Here are some examples of these styles, and an explanation of their meaning.

Code words in text are shown as follows: "We can include other contexts through the use of the `include` directive."

A block of code is set as follows:

```
public function _prepareLayout()
    {
      return parent::_prepareLayout();
    }
    public function getHelloworld()
    {
      return 'Hello world';
    }
```

When we wish to draw your attention to a particular part of a code block, the relevant lines or items are set in bold:

```
public function _prepareLayout()
    {
      return parent::_prepareLayout();
    }
    public function getHelloworld()
    {
      return 'Hello world';
    }
```

Any command-line input or output is written as follows:

```
# cp /usr/src/asterisk-addons/configs/cdr_mysql.conf.sample
    /etc/asterisk/cdr_mysql.conf
```

New terms and **important words** are shown in bold. Words that you see on the screen, in menus or dialog boxes for example, appear in the text like this: "clicking the **Next** button moves you to the next screen".

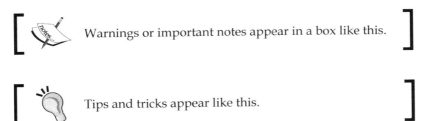

Warnings or important notes appear in a box like this.

Tips and tricks appear like this.

Reader feedback

Feedback from our readers is always welcome. Let us know what you think about this book—what you liked or may have disliked. Reader feedback is important for us to develop titles that you really get the most out of.

To send us general feedback, simply send an email to feedback@packtpub.com, and mention the book title via the subject of your message.

If there is a book that you need and would like to see us publish, please send us a note in the **SUGGEST A TITLE** form on www.packtpub.com or email suggest@packtpub.com.

 If there is a topic that you have expertise in and you are interested in either writing or contributing to a book on, see our author guide on www.packtpub.com/authors.

Customer support

Now that you are the proud owner of a Packt book, we have a number of things to help you to get the most from your purchase.

 Downloading the example code for the book
Visit http://www.packtpub.com/files/code/7249_Code.zip to directly download the example code.
The downloadable files contain instructions on how to use them.

Errata

Although we have taken every care to ensure the accuracy of our content, mistakes do happen. If you find a mistake in one of our books—maybe a mistake in the text or the code—we would be grateful if you would report this to us. By doing so, you can save other readers from frustration, and help us to improve subsequent versions of this book. If you find any errata, please report them by visiting http://www.packtpub.com/support, selecting your book, clicking on the **let us know** link, and entering the details of your errata. Once your errata are verified, your submission will be accepted and the errata added to any list of existing errata. Any existing errata can be viewed by selecting your title from http://www.packtpub.com/support.

Piracy

Piracy of copyright material on the Internet is an ongoing problem across all media. At Packt, we take the protection of our copyright and licenses very seriously. If you come across any illegal copies of our works, in any form, on the Internet, please provide us with the location address or web site name immediately so that we can pursue a remedy.

Please contact us at `copyright@packtpub.com` with a link to the suspected pirated material.

We appreciate your help in protecting our authors, and our ability to bring you valuable content.

Questions

You can contact us at `questions@packtpub.com` if you are having a problem with any aspect of the book, and we will do our best to address it.

1
Magento 1.3: PHP Developer's Guide

After developing a site or two in Magento, we would want to take our development a step ahead. Magento 1.3: PHP Developer's Guide is a book for those developers who want to work with the Magento e-commerce platform. In this book, we will be guided through the fundamentals of development with Magento.

If we're either frustrated with the "give you all the code" tutorials and articles online or actually really prefer them then, we'll find comfort in the code examples given in this book. Each code block in the book is followed by a detailed piece-by-piece explanation of what each part of the code does. This way, we can get information about not just the functionality, but also learn about the inner workings of the code being implemented.

Practical knowledge focused on common requirements of any Magento development is gained in this book, in both the day-to-day environment, as well as casual pick-it-up-when-you-need-it situations. This book will add to our development knowledge, once we go through it thoroughly. We will learn the following:

- Bettering our standards - We'll begin to understand the standards of Magento development and learn the outline of Magento itself, following through to the core architecture.
- Providing an extremely solid base for development. - The solid base, built by reading this book and following the practical examples in this book, will enable us to experiment with Magento's functionality and extend it in ways unheard of previously.
- The ability to solve frequently occurring issues. - The time spent developing with Magento will help us in resolving frequently occurring issues. We'll learn to build payment and shipping modules. We'll also learn how to interact with the Magento Core API and importing/exporting data for our websites.

Extending Magento

In this book, we'll be extending Magento in four core areas throughout. These can be broken down into the following:

- Extensions of existing functionality with new modules that extend the functionality of Magento beyond the module's capability.

- Brand new pieces of functionality that will seamlessly integrate with Magento's infrastructure to introduce new features to the overall Magento system, beyond its core base.

- Payment and Shipping methods which implement either special formulas for processing payment and shipping, or integrate with existing gateways of other providers.

- Wordpress CMS integration to implement Wordpress data into a Magento store, both through a sidebar display block and a blog using our Magento theme template.

With each of these methods for extending Magento, we'll go through how existing modules within Magento do it and how we can too, building real-world examples as we go along.

Practical examples will be used and explained block by block as we go along. Every piece of code is run through to start, allowing us to skim through the chapters when we need the code in a hurry. It is also then backtracked over to ensure that proper understanding and meaningful explanation is given to every block that is placed into our modules or scripts. This ensures that no function is unknown, once the code it written.

We'll extend Magento throughout this book, without touching any of the core files in the installation. This means that the methods taught in this book and those used throughout this book, will not affect the core installation of Magento. When upgrading, we won't need to worry about module malfunctioning.

Core development functionality coverage

In this book, we will cover several topics that we encounter when programming with Magento. These vary from functionality you will touch upon in every single site you build or maintain that is using Magento to functionality that will be touched upon not quite so much, but is equally as important to be aware of when developing with Magento.

Core principles of development

We'll learn everything from building modules that are not touching upon Magento's core installation, to the file structure of Magento, to the core principles of development with Magento in this book.

System maintenance

Important factors such as upgrading Magento and installed modules, backing up internal system data, and fixing commonly occurring issues will be covered in this book.

Payment and shipping module development

We'll learn how to build both payment and shipping modules while reading this book. These will expand upon Magento's base and provide additional functionality.

Module development

We will build several modules in this book, from basic modules that bring additional features to Magento, to fully featured extensions that manage data in the backend of Magento, as well as having dynamic frontends and their own dedicated URL structure for display.

Data portability and interaction

Probably the biggest factor in choosing any content management system has to, be whether or not we can get the data in or out of the system. Whether or not it will integrate with our existing systems is also a large concern.

In this book, we'll cover mass importing and updating of data via Excel documents and the built-in Core API. These will allow integration with existing backend or internal systems. We'll also cover how to integrate Magento with third-party content management systems.

Chapter overview

The chapters in this book vary greatly in terms of what they teach, to ensure that as many topics are covered as possible. This ensures that in depth knowledge of development is gained from them.

The following topics on Magento development will be covered:

Installing, upgrading, and preparing for development

We'll start by walking through the server requirements for installing Magento and proceed onto how to check manually and how to check automatically using a prepared script that Magento provides for you to check hosting environments prior to installing Magento on them.

Installing Magento manually will be covered step by step, from downloading Magento to uploading the contents of the zip file to our server and going through the installation right to the end. Upgrading will then be covered to ensure that Magento installations are kept up to date with the latest updates released by Varien.

We'll walk through how to perform both these actions through a Secure Shell connection to be able to use your root server access to speed up the upgrade and installation process as well as automate it. SVN (Subversion) users will be able to keep the installation updated using Magento's repository. Overall, this chapter will make sure Magneto's installation and upgrade process can fit into our workflow and suit our hosting environment setup.

System architecture

In this chapter we'll run through the architecture behind Magento's system, covering the core file structure and through to how the template system works. This will be important to understanding Magento as a whole and placing our files in the right place when beginning development. It will help break down the barriers between approaching Magento for the first time and developing your first project that plague most developers.

We'll learn more about the Zend Framework and how it powers Magento's core architecture. This will be explained for a better understanding of Magento's structure.

We'll also go through the best methods for backing up data within Magento, to make sure you're covered before doing anything drastic with your installation and that any data is safe from loss going forward.

Shipping modules

Every Magento installation uses Shipping modules to give the user the option of how their items are delivered to them once they are paid for. In this chapter, we'll be learning how to build a basic shipping module for Magento that will form a module skeleton of functions which can be used in further development of shipping modules. We'll go through what other shipping modules have done and what's possible when building shipping modules for Magento.

Proceeding from there, we'll build a basic shipping module with a few methods applied to it, which will put what we've learned into practice.

Payment modules

Payment modules are vital in Magento, and we'll walk through how to build a basic skeleton of a payment module, in the payment module chapter. From this, we'll learn how they are structured and how to build the base before advancing ahead to something better.

We'll learn how to add basic events to our payment module to advance it towards a fuller integration than expected from a basic module.

Basic module creation and implementation

We'll learn the basics of module creation to build a simple featured-products module implementation which features products on a per category basis. This will outline the principles of structure and implementation of a basic module development useful for further development.

In addition to this, we'll run through some quick tips that will help with Magento development. We'll try to resolve a few common issues that arise during development.

Fully-featured module development with administration panels

With this chapter, we'll be delving deeper into Magento by building a basic brand management module. This will manage brands and display their details, which will be output in a dynamic template that has its own dynamic URL.

This chapter will show the implementation and functioning of the administration section inside Magento, which allows management of our module from the backend. We'll then use this module and its backend for getting a dedicated URL on the frontend and a dynamic output for the managed data.

We'll also go through using the Module Creator script, put together by `<credit>` to speed up our module creation process in the future. This will cover the base installation of the Module Creator script and how to put it to use.

Integration of third-party CMS

In this chapter, we'll be covering third-party CMS integration, the possibilities and the helping aids in integrating our favourite CMS into Magento for data portability. We'll use Wordpress as a core example and implement Wordpress into Magento using a popular extension.

We'll also walk through other options available for implementation with other CMS. These CMS include Drupal, Typo3, Expression Engine, and Joomla!; the overview and options available for each are described in the chapter.

Magento's core API

Every installation of Magento comes with an available data API for external scripts and internal scripts to interact with the Magento installation's data. We'll walk through how it can be used, setting up the API within an installation, and handling error feedback when it occurs during usage.

We'll learn about the available methods which the API offers and see examples of what can be done with basic outlay of what comes with a default Magento installation. Along with this, there will be practical examples of how to put the API to use with these calls to produce something viable (such as a script) to be used in the future.

Importing and exporting data

Managing data is an import aspect of Magento, and in this chapter we'll be discussing the built-in methods of mass customer, order, and product data available within Magento.

We'll go through how to import externally located files for retrieving and storing information from and to external sources, to mass update or export information with our Magento installation.

Summary

This book aims to provide us with a solid foundation of knowledge to develop a site upon by using Magento. The ideas gained by reading this book will enable us to use Magento to build something advanced.

The internal functioning of Magento will be explained in depth, along with extending the present functions. This book will help us in developing our ideas into and onto Magento's default installation.

2
Installing/Upgrading Magento and Preparing for Development

In this chapter, we will get everything setup in order to begin development with Magento. We will go through the four methods that are available when installing and upgrading our Magento installation, so that we're able to pick the one that best suits our path in development.

Please note: upgrading is not a requirement of installing Magento, but it will be covered in this chapter. This will ensure that we're able to upgrade the system, as necessary, when an upgrade is released for Magento. Upgrading ensures that the system remains bug free and secure.

Requirements

The following are the specifications that Magento requires in order to run at a base level. These are not the requirements for tens of thousands of products but will have Magento running a small installation. These specifics are copied directly from the requirements page on MagentoCommerce.com for maximum reliability:

- Supported operating systems
  - Linux x86, x86-64
- Supported Web Servers:
  - Apache 1.3.x
  - Apache 2.0.x
  - Apache 2.2.x

- Supported Browsers:
    - Microsoft Internet Explorer 6 and above
    - Mozilla Firefox 2.0 and above
    - Apple Safari 2.x
    - Google Chrome
    - Adobe Flash browser plug-in should be installed
- PHP Compatibility:
    - 5.2.0 and above
    - Required extensions:
    - PDO_MySQL
    - simplexml
    - mcrypt
    - hash
    - GD
    - DOM
    - iconv
    - SOAP (if Webservices API is to be used)
    - Safe_mode off
    - Memory_limit 32M or more
- MySQL:
    - 4.1.20 or newer
    - InnoDB storage engine
- SSL:
    - If HTTPS is used to work in the admin, SSL certificate should be valid. Self-signed SSL certificates are not supported
- Server - hosting - setup:
    - Ability to run scheduled jobs (crontab) with PHP 5
    - Ability to override options in .htaccess files

 We can keep up to date with the latest system requirements for Magento at the following URL: http://www.magentocommerce.com/system-requirements

To check that our development setup meets the system requirements (mentioned previously), Magento Commerce provides an automated solution that can be downloaded and placed on our server. The script can be downloaded from: `http://www.magentocommerce.com/_media/magento-check.zip`. After downloading this file, we must unzip it into a directory and upload the contents into our directory in which we want to install Magento. Then, we simply navigate our browser to the URL, appending it with `/magento-check.php` to run the file. This file starts with a `<?` PHP short tag, as opposed to a `<?php` PHP opening tag. We'll have to change that in the file, if our server does not have short tags enabled on the PHP configuration.

> The script's URL will appear on the download script's knowledge base entry: `http://www.magentocommerce.com/knowledge-base/entry/how-do-i-know-if-my-server-is-compatible-with-magento`.

When you run the PHP file to check the requirements and your server meets them, you'll see a screen along the lines of the following:

Congratulations! Your server meets the requirements for Magento.

- You have **PHP 5.2.0** (or greater)
- Safe Mode is **off**
- You have **MySQL 4.1.20** (or greater)
- You have the **curl** extension
- You have the **dom** extension
- You have the **gd** extension
- You have the **hash** extension
- You have the **iconv** extension
- You have the **mcrypt** extension
- You have the **pcre** extension
- You have the **pdo** extension
- You have the **pdo_mysql** extension
- You have the **simplexml** extension

If the Magento check fails, the server administrator or web host is to be consulted for advice.

> For instructions on dealing with other operating systems, there are plenty of Magento Commerce Wiki entries available at `http://www.magentocommerce.com/download/noregister`.
> Just click the **How to Get Started** tab.

Once a Congratulations message (similar to the one in the previous screenshot) is displayed, then we're ready to proceed onto the installation.

Types of installation

We'll go through all the methods available for the installation of Magento, to extend our knowledge. It's not necessary to know all of them, but it will help us discover our preferred methods and the one which moulds itself to our development practices the best.

There are four methods of installation available for Magento:

- Manual — manually downloading and uploading all files needed
- Downloader — downloading a script for some of the files which when uploaded and run, will download the rest.
- SSH — connecting to the server via shell and running a set number of commands which will download, unzip, and set all the file permissions correctly for us
- Subversion (SVN) — checking out or exporting from the repository to our server, before committing to the local directory where we would like our installation

Manual

This method of installation is dubbed Manual, as we will have to do all the downloading and uploading ourselves. None of the other methods make us do this and will automate at least small parts of the process. Unfortunately, not everybody's server environment allows the use of the other methods for various reasons. So, the Manual method is vital for those stubborn or restricted hosting environments where we have no other choice.

Installing

We'll start by going to the Magento Commerce download page online, at `http://www.magentocommerce.com/download`.

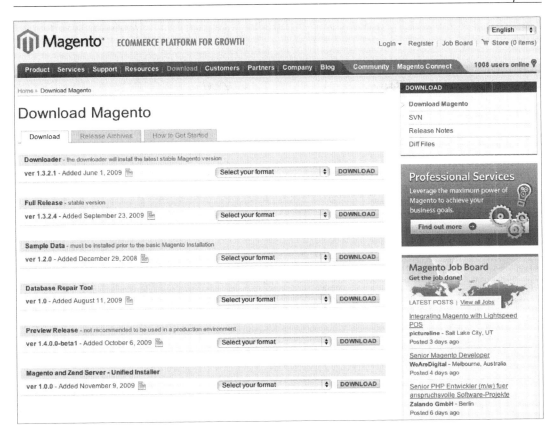

From here, we choose **Full Release** and download in the appropriate format. There isn't any difference in the formats apart from the size. If we're unsure about the format which our computer can unzip, then its better to simply choose the most universally compatible format, the .zip format.

Once we've downloaded our archive of the Magento files, we expand the archive and get our full listing of files, as shown in the following screenshot:

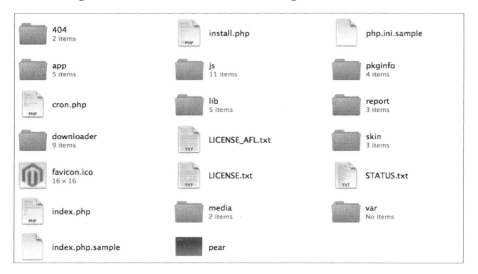

One thing to note about the directory structure is that it contains the downloader and the pear file for two of the other methods for installing/upgrading. So we're free to switch to other methods for upgrading, after an initial Manual install.

Once we've expanded the archive of files that we have downloaded, we connect to our FTP server, navigate to the folder where we want our Magento installation to reside in, and upload everything.

When the upload process finishes, we must ensure that the folders and contents of the folders (mentioned below) are set to 0755 in CHMOD permissions:

- /app/etc/
- /var/
- /media/

We proceed by navigating to the URL of our chosen install location. There are two ways to progress from here:

- By following the graphical interface and the instructions on-screen to complete the installation of Magento.
- By navigating to /app/etc/ and finding the local.xml.template file. We duplicate this file and save it as local.xml. Then we fill in all the details between the tags. This is best done after the first install of Magento, so that we can see how the data is formatted after the template is used by the graphical interface for populating data.

Those who choose the graphical interface option should see the following when navigating to the URL of our chosen Magento installation location:

The license agreement for Magento covers what we can and cannot do with the software. It's important to read it throughly (if we have the time) as it gives us a fantastic insight into the inner workings of the Open Source movement and how the licensing process works.

Version 1.5

 . Zip about 20 MB
 unzipped about 63 MB.

Presuming that we agree to abide by the terms, we then tick the box and click **Continue** to proceed to the next stage of the installation.

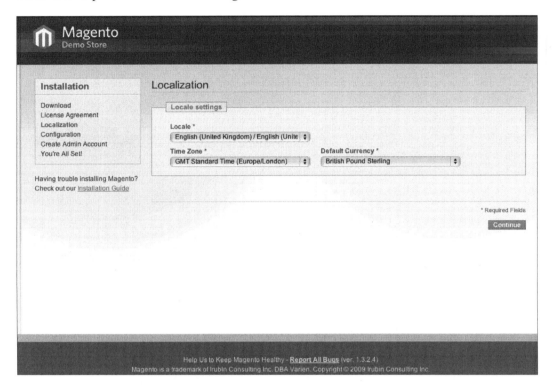

This screen allows us to set the default locale, the time zone, and the initial currency for our Magento installation. These can all be changed, once we go into the administration after installation finishes. However, it's best to set them right away so that we don't have to change them later. Clicking **Continue** after configuring these variables takes us onto the **Configuration** screen of the installation.

The previous screen is straightforward; all the information in it is about the Admin account, which we'll use to access our system. The only part to take particular notice of is the **Encryption Key** field at the bottom. It is advisable to leave it blank in the case of a standard installation. However, if we install a setup that corresponds with another on our server (for example, a development or a testing version of a site), then we will need to copy the previous key into the **Encryption Key** field.

Once we've finished this section, we'll see the standard Magento installation success screen that tells us our **Encryption Key**. It gives us links to both the backend and the frontend of our installation, in case we want to progress onto either.

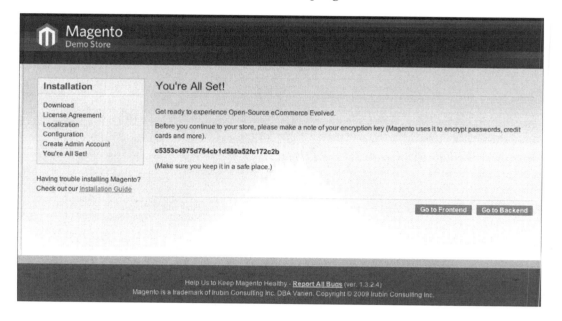

Upgrading

When an upgrade is required for our site, we can manually update Magento using the following routine. An upgrade is not required directly after an initial install.

To upgrade the installation—using the Manual method with a full package download—we have to:

- Back up our core files (for "just incase it goes wrong" purposes only)
  - Back up the database
  - Back up all code that we have modified ourselves (modules, themes, skins, and so on)
  - Back up our media directory, which contains all uploaded images for categories or products
  - Back up our /app/etc/local.xml file, which contains our database configuration and encryption key
- Upload all files from our downloaded full release file. We can either:
  - Skip overwriting the backed up files and upload everything else or

- ○ Overwrite all backed up files and then re-upload them to their appropriate directories
- Clear our /var/cache and /var/session directories to ensure no data from the previous install version lies around unwanted
- Point the browser to any page in the Magento installation to run the upgrade script from the previous version to the current version and we're done!

Downloader

The advantage of the downloader is that we have a much smaller initial download. Later the script can download the bigger files, saving the extra time taken to set up Magento. This reduces the initial download from between 40-50 MB to 1 MB and is especially useful for slower connections. It also means we can stay away from FTP when it comes to upgrading in the future, as the downloader also allows us to upgrade existing installations that have been installed using other methods.

Installing

To download from http://www.magentocommerce.com/download, we select the Downloader package. Expanding that displays a directory that looks similar to next screenshot:

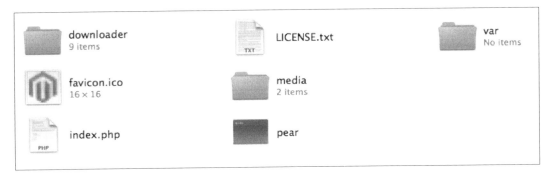

Next, we upload everything to the chosen Magento installation directory and load /downloader/ URL in our browser. A screen welcoming us to the downloader is displayed:

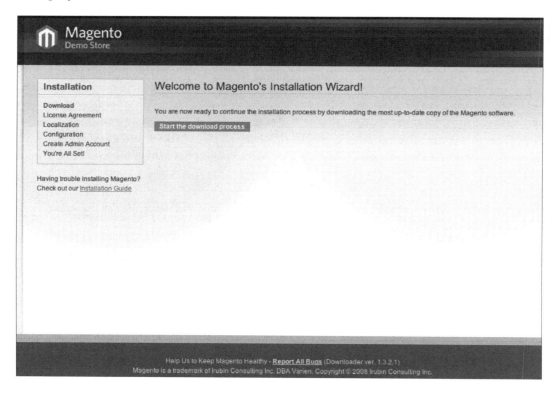

Once we click on **Start the download process**, we'll be presented with a screen that shows us the download progress. We must be patient, as it could take a long time before anything comes up. We should keep our browser window open and ensure that it isn't disrupted in any way. When it's done, the page will look similar to the next screenshot:

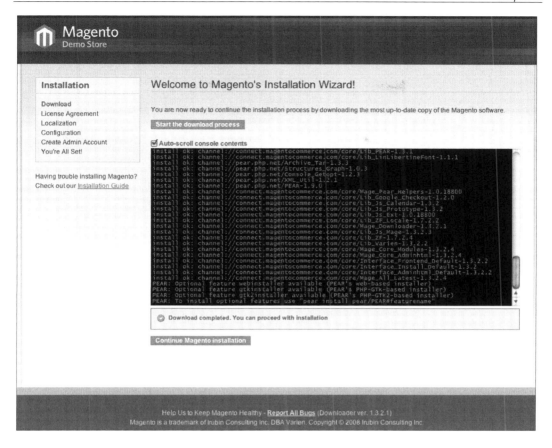

After clicking on **Continue Magento Installation** at the bottom of the page, we progress onto the standard GUI in order to complete the installation. We can refer to the previous section (Manual installation) to learn about installation using the standard GUI.

Upgrading

Once an update is available for Magento, we can load the `/downloader/` directory onto our chosen Magento installation URL. We are prompted with a login screen.

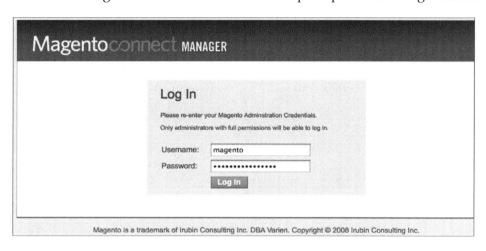

We type in our administration **Username** and **Password** for the chosen Magento installation into the boxes, after which, we're be allowed into the downloader interface.

Here we can install new extensions (should we want to), at the top of the page. Below, we find a **Check for Upgrades** button and a list of the extensions currently installed. We can select **re-install** or **un-install** actions from the drop-downs for each extension as we wish, and commit all the changes at once using the button at the bottom.

As we're upgrading, we would want to click on the **Check for Upgrades** button at the top. Once the page has refreshed from checking for upgrades, we'll see all the extensions that have available upgrades highlighted in the table.

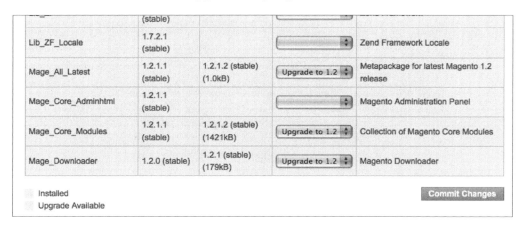

Select **Upgrade to...** from the drop-down, in the extensions you want to upgrade, and click **Commit Changes** at the bottom of the page. After doing this, a dialog area appears which shows the progress, similar to how the install dialog appeared for showing progress during installation.

We can access any URL in our Magento installation and all mySQL upgrades will take place to complete the upgrade.

SSH (Secure Shell)

SSH is the fastest of the four installations and upgrade options for Magento and a preferred choice of the four. It is command line only and enables us to do the entire process without the use of any GUI, besides the client that we use to run the commands. It is typically available only on dedicated hosting environments and will be available to those who have root access to the contents of their hosting server environment. The majority of shared hosting or reseller hosting will not provide SSH access or root access. VPS usually provide root access similar to dedicated hosting environments, but it's not standard everywhere.

For each of these stages, we must ensure that we're connected via SSH to our server, using the following command:

```
ssh username@server_address
```

Note that the server address can be a direct URL or the IP address of the server that we are connecting to. Afterwards, we will be prompted for our username's password. Once we have done that, we'll be logged in and can get to the planned installation's directory. The command to get there is:

```
cd /full/path/to/installation/directory/
```

We're ready to install/upgrade, once we're inside the directory of the chosen installation address.

Installing

Like the downloader, we will still need to run through the GUI after installation. However, this will be much quicker and we will get real time feedback on what is happening, once we start executing the commands.

The first line is spread over two lines due to the length of the URL from where the download is fetched. We have to insert that as a single command. We'll be installing version 1.3.2.4. We need to switch all occurrences of this version number with the most current version so that it installs the most recent version of Magento.

```
wget http://www.magentocommerce.com/downloads/assets/1.3.2.4/magento-1.3.2.4.tar.gz
tar -zxvf magento-1.3.2.4.tar.gz
mv magento/* magento/.htaccess .
chmod o+w var var/.htaccess app/etc
chmod -R o+w media
./pear mage-setup .
```

```
./pear install magento-core/Mage_All_Latest-stable
rm -rf downloader/pearlib/cache/* downloader/pearlib/download/*
rm -rf magento/ magento-1.3.2.4.tar.gz
```

Mac users should replace the line beginning with wget with the

following:

```
curl http://www.magentocommerce.com/downloads/assets/1.3.2.3/magento-
1.3.2.3.tar.gz > magento-1.3.2.3.tar.gz
```

From here, we can access our chosen Magento installation location via HTTP and follow the graphical user interface to complete the installation.

 There is a way to bypass the installation wizard, but it requires the reader to know all the correct variables to proceed into the required areas. Information on it can be found at: http://www.magentocommerce.com/wiki/groups/227/command_line_installation_wizard.

Upgrading

Upgrading is just as simple as installation. Go to the directory of the Magento installation you wish to upgrade and run the following:

```
./pear mage-setup .
./pear install magento-core/Mage_All_Latest
rm -rf downloader/pearlib/cache/* downloader/pearlib/download/*
```

After we've executed the previous command, the Magento installation will be upgraded. We'll just need to access it at its appropriate URL, as with the other methods, and all MySQL related updates will take place.

If we need to clear our cache and sessions, we can use the following command:

```
rm -rf var/cache/* var/session/*
```

SVN (Subversion Network)

For those unfamiliar with Subversion, there are numerous links in the Appendix where we can learn about what it is, what it does, and how it can be used on our platform of choice.

For those familiar with SVN already, there is an available SVN repository setup, if we want to use it. Those already trained in working with SVN will only need to know the following command to keep the installation up-to-date or to install it at another location:

`svn export http://svn.magentocommerce.com/source/branches/1.3`

There is also a `trunk` setup for versions in progress and in alpha testing, though it is advisable to not use it in any production environments. In case we want to test it, we can do so with the following command:

`svn export http://svn.magentocommerce.com/source/branches/1.3-trunk`

These commands relate to the 1.3 string of Magento, so for future versions you will need to replace the version number in the commands.

Summary

In this chapter, we've learned how to install and upgrade Magento in all four methods available to us. We can now do the following:

- Install/upgrade manually, by downloading/uploading all files and backing up the appropriate files we need to
- Install/upgrade via the downloader
- Install/upgrade via SSH
- Install/upgrade via SVN

In the next chapter, we will learn about the structure of Magento and the inner architecture that makes Magento work. This is key to understanding how to develop with it. Whether it is themes, skins, modules, or moving it from server to server, the next chapter will teach us how to handle Magento and where to find what we looking for when we need to.

3
Magento's Architecture

Magento has a wonderful architecture behind its system. It's a very strict architecture that relies on us knowing where the files should be placed and how to structure our templates and modules. But this is part of what makes Magento a great system, in that it enforces these standards.

Here in this chapter, we will learn about this architecture and how it applies to development with Magento. We will learn:

- Where everything is within Magento
- What all the base directory files and folders do
- The basics of how the template system works
- How modules work within the system
- How the Zend Framework fits into the equation
- The best methods for backing up Magento

Magento's base structure

The fundamental knowledge of Magento's architecture begins with its file structure. It's important to know what goes where by default, so that we may position our new files accordingly, especially in terms of ensuring that our development doesn't overwrite core files.

Base directory

The default installation contains the following files and directories in the
base directory:

- `.htaccess`
- `.htaccess.sample`
- `404` (directory)
- `app` (directory)
- `cron.php`
- `downloader` (directory)
- `favicon.ico`
- `index.php`
- `index.php.sample`
- `js` (directory)
- `lib` (directory)
- `LICENSE_AFL.txt`
- `LICENSE.txt`
- `media` (directory)
- `pear`
- `pkginfo` (directory)
- `report` (directory)
- `skin` (directory)
- `var` (directory)

Each of these files and directories has a different purpose. We'll go through them
to ensure that we understand the function of each. This will help us later, if ever
we need to find something specific, or when developing. It will also be helpful
when we'll be looking to place the files coming out of our new module into the
appropriate directory.

The function of each of the files in the base directory

The following is a run through of all the files in the base directory, to show us what they do:

- `.htaccess` — This file controls `mod_rewrite` for fancy URLs and sets configuration server variables (such as memory limit) and PHP maximum execution time, so that Magento can run better.

- `.htaccess.sample` — Works as a backup for `.htaccess`, so that we know the default `.htaccess` file (if ever we edit it and need to backtrack).

- `cron.php` — The file that should be executed as a `cron` job every few minutes to ensure that Magento's wide caching doesn't affect our server's performance.

- `favicon.ico` — Magento's default `favicon`; it's the small icon that appears in the toolbar of our browser.

- `index.php` — The main loader file for Magento and the file that initializes everything.

- `index.php.sample` — The base template for new `index.php` files, useful when we have edited the `index.php` file and need to backtrack.

- `LICENSE_AFL.txt` — It contains the Academic Free License that Magento is distributed under.

- `LICENSE.txt` — It contains the Open Software License that Magento is distributed under.

- `pear` — This controls all automatic updating via the downloader and SSH. This file is initialized and handles the updating of each individual module that makes up Magento.

- `php.ini` — A sample `php.ini` file for raw PHP server variables recommended when setting up Magento on our server. This should not be used as a complete replacement, but only as a guide to replace certain lines of the `php.ini` server file. It is useful when overriding these variables when `.htaccess` isn't enabled on our server.

The function of each of the folders in the base directory

The following is a run through of all the folders in the base directory to show us their contents:

- 404 — The default 404 template and skin storage folder for Magento.

- app — All code (modules), design (themes), configuration, and translation files are stored in this directory. This is the folder that we'll be working in extensively, when developing a Magento powered website. Also contained in this folder are the template files for the default administration theme and installation.

- downloader — The web downloader for upgrading and installing Magento without the use of SSH (covered in Chapter 2).

- js — The core folder where all JavaScript code included with the installation of Magento is kept. We will find all pre-compiled libraries of JavaScript here.

- lib — All PHP libraries used to put together Magento. This is the core code of Magento that ties everything together. The Zend Framework is also stored within this directory.

- media — All media is stored here. Primarily for images out of the box, this is where all generated thumbnails and uploaded product images will be stored. It is also the container for importing images, when using the mass import/export tools (that we'll go through in Chapter 10).

- pkginfo — Short form of package information, this directory contains text files that largely operate as debug files to inform us about changes when modules are upgraded in any way.

- report — The skin folder for the reports that Magento outputs when any error occurs.

- skin — All assets for themes are stored within this directory. We typically find images, JavaScript files, CSS files, and Flash files relating to themes, in this directory. However, it can be used to store any assets associated with a theme. It also contains the skin files for the installation of skins and administration templates.

- var — Typically where we will find all cache and generated files for Magento. We can find the cache, sessions (if storing as files), data exports, database backups, and cached error reports in this folder.

The template system architecture

The template architecture is broken into three areas—two for development of the theme and one for the containment of the assets:

- /app/design/frontend/default/<template_name>/
  - layout/—For all the XML files declaring which module tied functions should be called to which template files
  - template/—For all the templates processing the output that is passed from functions called from layout/ and structured into the final output to the user.
- /skin/frontend/default/<template_name>/—For the containment of all assets relating to our template, images, CSS, Flash, and JavaScript.

Structural blocks and content blocks

Each theme contains structural and content blocks. Structural blocks are the ones that lay out the theme into sections. Let's take a look at a three-column layout. The following are the structural blocks in a three-column layout:

- **header**
- **left**
- **content**
- **right**
- **footer**

Here's a visual representation of those structural blocks laid over the Magento demo store:

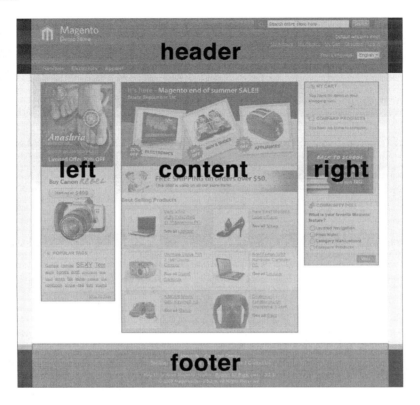

In each of the structural blocks, we then have content blocks that give each structural block its content for output to the browser. Let's take the **right** column; our content blocks set for this column on a standard theme could be:

- **mini cart**
- recently viewed products
- newsletter subscription block
- **poll**

Here we have a visual representation of these content blocks on top of the Magento demo store:

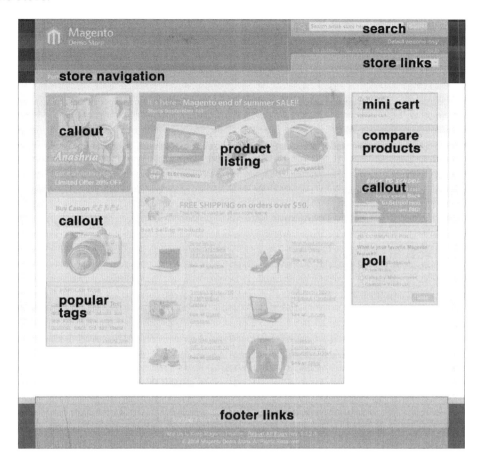

On receiving a request from a user connecting to our site to view the page:

1. Magento will load the structural areas
2. Each structural area will be processed through
3. Magento will gather the content blocks assigned to each structural area
4. It will then progress through the content block template for each structural area, to process the output
5. It sends all of this back as final output to the user, who then views the Magento page that was requested

XML layout files

To assign blocks to each of these structural blocks, Magento loads an XML layout file for each request. This XML layout file is called by the URL that the user is accessing on the site. It declares all modules that are to be loaded in each structural area of the site. On top of this, we have a `page.xml` file, which is the default loader for all pages on the site.

A layout XML file is typically structures as follows:

```
<default>
  <reference name="header">
    <block type="page/html_header" name="header" as="header">
      <block type="page/template_links" name="top.links"
            as="topLinks"/>
      <block type="page/switch" name="store_language"
            as="store_language"
            template="page/switch/languages.phtml"/>
      <block type="core/text_list" name="top.menu" as="topMenu"/>
    </block>
  </reference>
</default>
```

In the above code, we have:

- `<default>`—The handler for the URL, in this case default will load no matter what other handler is being initialized
- `<reference>`—The reference structure which calls the blocks in our theme
- `<block>`—A content block which defines the type of block and the template which will process the block's outgoing data in the system

In addition to this, Magento uses actions within blocks for functions which need to process the data that is input to them, for example adding CSS stylesheets:

```
<block type="page/html_head" name="head" as="head">
  <action method="addCss">
    <stylesheet> css/menu.css </stylesheet>
  </action>
  <action method="addCss">
    <stylesheet> css/clears.css </stylesheet>
  </action>
```

```
<action method="addItem">
  <type>js</type>
  <name>varien/iehover-fix.js</name>
  <params/>
  <if>lt IE 7</if>
</action>
<action method="addCss">
  <stylesheet>css/print.css</stylesheet>
  <params>media="print"</params>
</action>
  <action method="addCss">
    <stylesheet> css/print.css </stylesheet>
    <params> media="print" </params>
  </action>
</block>
```

We'll notice that there are several tags within the action method tag. These are processed into an array and then passed through the action method="" parameter, in this case addCss. This function then places the input into an output, ready for its appropriate template.

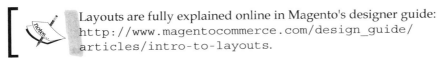

Layouts are fully explained online in Magento's designer guide: http://www.magentocommerce.com/design_guide/articles/intro-to-layouts.

Hierarchical file processing

When creating new themes, we do not have to worry about copying all the theme and skin files from the default theme over to our new one. Let's presume that we have an additional theme called new_theme, alongside our default theme. Our theme calls files called logo.gif and image.gif on one of its pages.

The themes that we have contain the following files in their skin's images directory:

default	new_theme
logo.gif	logo.gif
image.gif	
test.gif	

Magento would process this main requesting `logo.gif` and `image.gif`. As `new_theme` is our current active theme, it will pull `logo.gif` from there., However, as `image.gif` does not exist in `new_theme`, Magento would grab that from `default`. So now, it works like this:

Requested file	Theme it will come from
logo.gif	new_theme
image.gif	default

Similarly, if `test.gif` were called in our template then it would come from the default theme. If we upload an image called `test.gif` to the image directory of `new_theme`, then it would immediately come from there instead.

This applies to all files for themes in Magento, which include the following:

- Templates
- Layout XML files
- Anything in the theme skin folders

 Magento's template architecture and hierarchy is also explained online in the designer's guide to Magento: `http://www.magentocommerce.com/design_guide`

Modules and how they work within the system

Magento primarily works on a base of modules. All functionality is divided up into modules that make up the system overall. It's important to understand what each module does and how to go about adding modules to the system, in order to understand the architecture of modules themselves.

Distribution of the modules between directories

All modules are located within the /app/code/ directory. Directories are commonly referred to as codePools. There are three possible locations for all modules that relate to the system. They are all split by type to prevent any confusion:

- community—For community-distributed extensions, usually those that we have installed through Magento Connect or have downloaded from a source, other than our own. Anything installed through Magento Connect will be installed here automatically.

- core—Reserved for core Magento modules, so that we cannot directly overwrite or interfere with them. We keep our modules out of core to avoid any conflict with the core modules or any future updates. Anything from a Magento upgrade or any new Magento modules will go into this directory.

- Local—This is where we should be placing our modules when they are either under local development or are not distributed among the community. It's best to keep anything that we develop in this directory, so as to not interfere with the core or community modules. Nothing will be automatically installed here, unless we have physically uploaded it.

Modules included with Magento

Included modules in the core folder of default Magento installation are as follows:

- Mage_Admin
- Mage_AdminNotification
- Mage_Api
- Mage_Backup
- Mage_Bundle
- Mage_Catalog
- Mage_CatalogIndex
- Mage_CatalogInventory
- Mage_CatalogRule
- Mage_CatalogSearch
- Mage_Checkout
- Mage_Cms
- Mage_Contacts
- Mage_Core

- Mage_Cron
- Mage_Customer
- Mage_Dataflow
- Mage_Directory
- Mage_Downloadable
- Mage_Eav
- Mage_GiftMessage
- Mage_GoogleAnalytics
- Mage_GoogleBase
- Mage_GoogleCheckout
- Mage_GoogleOptimizer
- Mage_Install
- Mage_Log
- Mage_Media
- Mage_Newsletter
- Mage_Page
- Mage_Paygate
- Mage_Payment
- Mage_Paypal
- Mage_PaypalUk
- Mage_Poll
- Mage_ProductAlert
- Mage_Rating
- Mage_Reports
- Mage_Review
- Mage_Rss
- Mage_Rule
- Mage_Sales
- Mage_SalesRule
- Mage_Sendfriend
- Mage_Shipping
- Mage_Sitemap
- Mage_Tag
- Mage_Tax

- Mage_Usa
- Mage_Weee
- Mage_Wishlist

Setting up the folder structure of a module

Let's presume that we want to set up a module's folder structure, ready for development. Our module's core folders will be placed in /app/code/local/Book/Example/.

These folders will primarily be used for storing our code that makes the module work. The folder structure breaks down as follows:

- Block/
- controllers/
- etc/
- Model/
    ○ Mysql4/
    ○   Book/
- sql/
    ○ book_setup/

Typically, developers will pick or choose each folder, depending on whether or not they're going to use it within their module.

Note that Model/Mysql4/Book/ has its first letter in uppercase, whereas sql/book_setup/ does not. We must be sure to keep this the same way throughout our development.

Template files for the frontend of our module will be stored as follows:

- XML files will be stored in /app/design/frontend/<interface>/<theme>/layout/example/
- Output files will be stored in /app/design/frontend/<interface>/<theme>/template/example/

Any admin template files for the frontend of our module will be stored as follows:

- XML files will be stored in /app/design/adminhtml/<interface>/<theme>/layout/example/
- Output files will be stored in /app/design/adminhtml/<interface>/<theme>/template/example/

Here's a breakdown of what each folder is for:

- `Block/` — For processing of all display blocks called by the system for the module. These are controllers that will be called in the XML layout files within a theme, in order to display something.

- `controllers/` — Our controllers that support the application and structurally keep things together.

- `etc/` — Configuration files for the module, for declaring things such as the default options when installed and declaring all blocks, models, and install/ upgrade actions.

- `Model/` — For placement of all models to support controllers in the module.

- `sql/` — SQL actions when the module is installed/upgraded/uninstalled.

Zend Framework and its role within Magento

Magento (at its raw PHP base) is built on the Zend Framework. From the database class to the handling of URLs, Magento is in its raw form, with Zend Framework doing all the work. Alongside this, Varien has built several core modules on top of the Zend Framework, in order to tie it altogether into the system as we know it.

What is Zend Framework

Zend Framework's official site best describes the framework as follows:

> *Zend Framework (ZF) is an open source framework for developing web applications and services with PHP 5. ZF is implemented using 100% object-oriented code. The component structure of ZF is somewhat unique; each component is designed with few dependencies on other components. This loosely coupled architecture allows developers to use components individually. We often call this a "use-at-will" design.*

While they can be used separately, Zend Framework components in the standard library form a powerful and extensible web application framework when combined. ZF offers a robust, high performance MVC implementation, a database abstraction that is simple to use, and a forms component that implements HTML form rendering, validation, and filtering so that developers can consolidate all of these operations using one easy-to-use, object-oriented interface. Other components, such as Zend_Auth and Zend_Acl, provide user authentication and authorization against all common credential stores. Still others implement client libraries to simply access to the most popular web services available. Whatever your application needs are, you're likely to find a Zend Framework component that can be used to dramatically reduce development time with a thoroughly tested foundation.

How Zend Framework works

The Zend Framework (at its core) is designed to be used as a package or separate modules. This (among other features) makes it unique, as most other frameworks are designed to be used plainly as frameworks or not at all.

However, the Zend Framework comes with classes that allow us to use it as a standalone framework and develop with it as one. Instead of being delivered with a preset amount of directories and layout for developers, it only suggests a layout for our files. This means that we can adapt the framework to meet our current workflow and choose how much we adapt the workflow to fit the framework.

It's role and effect in Magento

The Zend Framework allows Magento to focus on the core issues at hand. It removes a lot of the work on the database and core structural classes and puts the work towards fixing and adding to core modules of Magento.

Most importantly it gives developers a standard approach to development that they can move across and apply to Magento. The standard development practices help greatly in adopting Magento as a platform and make it easier for developers having experience with Zend Framework to adapt to Magento.

More information on learning the Zend Framework and resources can be found at the back of this book in the Appendix attached. Its official site is located at: http://framework.zend.com/.

Backing up Magento's data

It's important to know how to back up our site, to ensure that our installation's data is not lost (if ever things go bad).

It is recommended to back up our Magento installation:

- Regularly as a base to ensure that there are incremental backups of our system
- Before installing new modules or themes from Magento Connect
- When developing modules
- Before upgrading our system

Backing up the files

We will need to back up all the files relating to the Magento installation, when backing up our system. Two of the ways in which this can be done are given below.

Manually

Manually, we are able to download all the files of the installation to our hard drive. This is the longest method of backing up the files and is the most foolproof method available.

Using SSH

Using SSH, we're able to vastly speed up the duration of backing up the servers. We can do this in two ways:

- Zipping up all files, if the server has it enabled
- Copying all files to another directory

Both of these depend on whether or not our server has SSH. So if this isn't available to us, then we cannot use these methods.

Both of these methods require us to connect to our server via SSH first and then use the cd command to get to the directory (which Magento is installed in), before running the commands.

Zipping up all files

This will create a `zip` file of our entire Magento installation's files and folders called `magento_archive.zip`.

```
tar cf magento_archive.tar *
```

To `untar` this archive, extract the files afterwards:

```
tar -xvf yourfilename.tar
```

We can then move this to another directory of our choice using the mv command:

```
mv magento_archive.zip /path/to/new/destination/
```

Copying all files to another directory

We run the following command to copy all files (as they are) into another directory on our server. We'll replace the full path with the path to the desired directory, into which we want to copy all the files.

```
cp -R * /path/to/new/destination/
```

Backing up the database

We'll need to back up the database as part of our Magento backup. Let's go through how.

Using the system itself

Magento comes with a built-in method for backing up our installation and keeping several backups logged, in case we want to download older backups at any time. It can be found in the **System** menu under **Tools**:

The initial screen will be similar to the next screenshot:

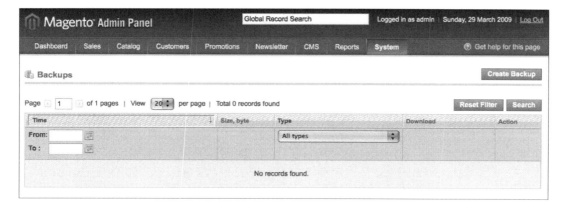

cron this?

To create a backup via the **System** panel, all we need to do is click on **Create Backup** in the upper-right of the screen and wait for it to finish:

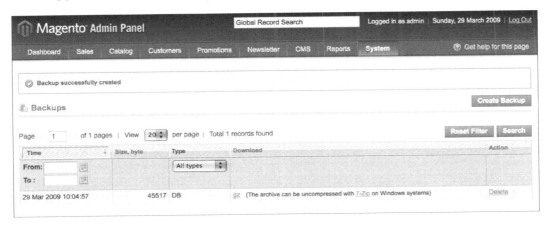

The process of creating a backup can take quite a while (especially for bigger databases), so we will need to keep an eye on our server's memory limits and PHP execution limits. These are set in our .htaccess file on runtime, but some servers will only run the defaults and not allow them to be overridden. If we encounter a white screen instead of the success message (shown in the previous screen), then the problem is either memory limit or execution time limit. We will need to increase them ourselves or contact our web host.

Once the backup is completed, however, we'll be able to find it in our /var/backups/ folder. They will be named by timestamp and the highest numbered filename will be the last to be backed up.

Using phpMyAdmin

The most common back up solution is phpMyAdmin, and some people prefer it over any built-in method. To export via phpMyAdmin, we:

1. Navigate to the database
2. Switch to the **export** tab
3. Select all tables and **SQL** as the export type
4. Under **options** on the right-hand side select **Disable foreign key checks**
5. Select **save as file** at the very bottom of the page
6. If we want to match the compression type of Magento's output, select **gzipped** as our compression method
7. Click the **Go** button to export

This will give us an SQL file, which we can then import at a later date back into an empty database and restore our data.

Summary

In this chapter, we've learned the following:

- How Magento's folder structure and files are laid out
- What each of the base directory's folders and files do
- How the template system works
- How modules work within Magento
- About the Zend Framework and how it benefits Magento
- How best to go about backing up Magento and when to go about it

Further to this chapter, I want you to read the Magento designer's guide and the Zend Framework documentation and examples. There are also a very good group of links for you to read through in the Appendix at the back of this book. These will increase your knowledge of the Magento architecture and benefit you throughout this book.

Shipping Modules in Magento

In this chapter, we will apply our newfound knowledge of Magento's core architecture (that we learned in the previous chapter) and apply it to one of the fundamental building blocks of Magento, its shipping module.

Here, we will learn how to create a shipping module, so that we can develop our own when the need arises. By the end of this chapter we will:

- Know where to find shipping modules that others have produced
- Know how to put together a basic shipping module and know what values pertain to what information
- Be able to create our own methods for calculation or handling shipping with Magento

What shipping modules do

Shipping modules are used to define the handling of the order, before it goes through the payment method section of the order process. They take the order itself and decide how to go about charging and delivering it to the customer. Magento takes the order through each shipping module that is installed and active in the system. Each shipping module is then able to process the order currently in the cart and present any available options to the user, from what it sees in the order.

For example: we have a shipping module in our system that provides free delivery to people located within the UK and ordering over £40. Let's presume that we are ordering £50 worth of goods and are located within the UK. When the order is sent through this module, it checks whether or not the user is in the UK and the order total is over £40. If these conditions are met, (which our order does), then we are presented with a free delivery option, among others, to choose during our order process.

This is a very simple version of what a shipping module can do. The full range of what can be done using shipping modules can be grasped by looking at **Shipping Modules** on Magento Connect and finding what it has on offer. Here's a small range of what has been made public:

- **Royal Mail UK, EU, and Worldwide Shipping module** — For calculation and handling of all of Royal Mail's shipping methods using weight and distance. This module sends key product information to Royal Mail via their API, authenticating with information that the Magento store administrator has input, and outputs pricing for various shipping options on the current order.

- **Regional Free Shipping module** — Gives the Magento administrator the option to allow free shipping by region, instead of by country. This provides a choice to the store administrator of breaking down free shipping further than country. For example, this would be good for someone who runs a store based in Nottingham that wants to reward local customers in the East Midlands, as opposed to simply giving free shipping to the entire United Kingdom.

- **Basic Store Pickup Shipping module** — Enables customers to choose between picking up the item themselves and having it delivered to them. This is advantageous for companies which use Magento and have a physical store presence with stock held.

 Magento Connect can be accessed at the following URL: `http://www.magentocommerce.com/magento-connect`.

The three core types of shipping module can be summarized in the following:

- Third-party API and/or web service integration. For integration with existing couriers that have web-based APIs or web services that offer the same for organization of your shipping. Many existing services make an API available to us for integrating into Magento. We should check Magento Connect for any existing modules that others have created.

- Using customer data to provide unique calculations and opportunities to certain users. Anything that the customer puts in it while checking out can be used for this type of module.

- Shipping methods that involve a physical store or location for additional options that compliment others. We could theoretically build up a set of stores under the Magento store company's business. We could then link them up with local computers at the locations and use the shipping module to check for stocks at each location. We should do that before suggesting the store as a location for the user to be able to pick up the item.

How to begin with a shipping module

Here we'll be learning about how to begin with a shipping module. This is the skeletal structure of a shipping module that we can use as a template for any shipping module which we create. We will also be using it to create a very basic shipping module at the end of this chapter.

For the purpose of following this tutorial, we will be creating all files in /app/code/ local/MagentoBook/ShippingModule/, which will be the base directory for all files created (from this point onwards). We must make sure that this directory and sub-directory are set up before continuing onwards. This means that if the file is declared to be /hello/world.php, we place this on the end of our initial base address and it becomes /app/code/local/MagentoBook/ShippingModule/hello/ world.php

Please start by creating the directory MagentoBook in /app/code/local/ and a sub-directory within that called ShippingModule, creating the directory structure /MagentoBook/ShippingModule/.

The configuration files

We create /app/code/local/MagentoBook/ShippingModule/etc/config.xml in our module's folder. Here, we'll place the following code which will declare our new module for use, make it depend on Mage_Shipping being enabled, set it at version 0.1.0 and allow it to use the existing global database connection which is set up for our store.

```
<?xml version="1.0"?>
<config>

  <modules>
    <MagentoBook_ShippingModule>
      <version>0.1.0</version>
      <depends>
        <Mage_Shipping />
      </depends>
    </MagentoBook_ShippingModule>
```

```
      </modules>
      <global>
        <models>
          <shippingmodule>
            <class>MagentoBook_ShippingModule_Model</class>
          </shippingmodule>
        </models>

        <resources>
          <shippingmodule_setup>
            <setup>
              <module>MagentoBook_ShippingModule</module>
            </setup>
            <connection>
              <use>core_setup</use>
              </connection>
          </shippingmodule_setup>
        </resources>
      </global>
      <default>
        <carriers>
          <shippingmodule>
            <model>MagentoBook/carrier_ShippingModule</model>
          </shippingmodule>
        </carriers>
      </default>
    </config>
```

Let's walk back through this code and go over what each individual section does.

We start by defining our XML header tag for the file, to ensure that it is accepted as an XML file when read by the XML parsing class in the system.

```
<?xml version="1.0"?>
```

We define the <config> tag, to ensure that everything within it is read as configuration variables to be loaded into Magento's configuration for whatever we define internally within this tag.

```
<config>
```

We define the <modules> tag, so that we're setting configuration variables for modules defined within this tag.

```
<modules>
  <MagentoBook_ShippingModule>
```

We set the module's version number to `0.1.0`, to supply Magento with versioning for the module in the future, if we update and need to perform statements within the update portion of the module, so as to execute above a certain version number.

```
<version>0.1.0</version>
```

We have to make sure that our module cannot be activated, or possibly run, without the `Mage_Shipping` core shipping handler and module activated. This is vital because the module being a shipping module is simply going to cause fatal errors without the parent `Mage_Shipping` module providing the helper functions needed internally.

```
<depends>
  <Mage_Shipping />
</depends>
```

Next, we close off our module declaration tag and modules tag.

```
    </MagentoBook_ShippingModule>
</modules>
```

We set up our `<global>` tag to define global assets to Magento.

```
<global>
```

Next, we define the `<models>` tag to define global models to the system and for setting up our module's default model to be one of those global models which is automatically loaded.

```
<models>
  <shippingmodule>
    <class>MagentoBook_ShippingModule_Model</class>
  </shippingmodule>
</models>
```

We define the `<resources>` tag, so that we can configure the database resources available to the module within the system.

```
<resources>
```

Defining the <resources> tag allows us to include a setup file with our module that accesses the database. This helps if we need to load in any variables (such as default table rate rules) for our module, or for loading additional data required locally by the module, when calculating the shipping rates.

```
<shippingmodule_setup>
  <setup>
    <module>MagentoBook_ShippingModule</module>
  </setup>
```

Here, we'll use the core database connection (the default one), and ensure that we do not overwrite the database connection set up for this particular module.

```
<connection>
  <use>core_setup</use>
    </connection>
```

We close off all tag pairs, besides <config>, that have been opened at this point.

```
    </shippingmodule_setup>
  </resources>
</global>
```

Finally, we end the configuration file with a declaration that our module is a shipping module and should be processed as one, within the system. This will register the module to the system, so that it can actually display shipping methods to the user on checkout. Without this, nothing will be returned to the user from this module.

```
<default>
  <carriers>
    <shippingmodule>
      <model>MagentoBook/carrier_ShippingModule</model>
    </shippingmodule>
  </carriers>
</default>
```

We close the <config> tag to end the XML configuration file.

```
</config>
```

After we've done this, we need to declare our module to Magento by creating a configuration file in /app/etc/modules/MagentoBook_ShippingModule.xml.

Next, we place the following code in our new configuration file, to allow this module to interact with Magento and be turned on/off under the **System Configuration** menu:

```
<?xml version="1.0"?>
<config>
  <modules>
    <MagentoBook_ShippingModule>
      <active>true</active>
      <codePool>local</codePool>
    </MagentoBook_ShippingModule>
  </modules>
</config>
```

We break this file down into the individual lines:

```
<?xml version="1.0"?>
```

The `<config>` wrapper tag defines the XML to be read, as a configuration of something inside Magento.

```
<config>
```

The `<modules>` wrapping tag defines this as a module to Magento.

```
<modules>
```

The next tag is used for defining that this is the configuration of a module entitled `<MagentoBook_ShippingModule>` and for applying the settings inside the tag to the module:

```
<MagentoBook_ShippingModule>
```

We make sure that it's active by default (this will be overwritten when activated/deactivated in the Magento administrative back-end).

```
<active>true</active>
```

The `<code pool>` tag is used for keeping this module in our local module's directory.

```
<codePool>local</codePool>
```

Closing tags are for closing the XML tags that we started the `<config>` tag with.

```
    </MagentoBook_ShippingModule>
  </modules>
</config>
```

 codePools are explained in full detail in Chapter 3, *Magento's Architecture* earlier in this book starting on page 47.

Now that we have the configuration set up, to allow the module to be managed within Magento and versioning control to allow for upgrades in the future, we can progress onto the module itself. It also means that we can now turn our module on/off within the administration. To do this, we go to **System | Configuration**, then to **Advanced** under the **Advanced** heading on the left-hand side. Once here, we will be presented with **Enable/Disable** dropdowns for each module installed in the system.

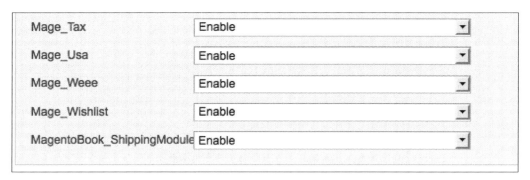

We'll set the dropdown for our module to **Disable** until we have completed the adaptor model and administration setup. This will prevent the module from crashing the system, while it is incomplete. We will re-activate the module once we're ready to see the output.

The adaptor model

The adaptor model handles the core functionality behind our shipping module. From its name, we can guess that it adapts what we have into a real module that works and functions. This is something that both shipping and payment modules have.

This is where all the calculations happen and where everything will be coded. The coding is done behind the scenes to handle the shipping methods and the rates returned to the user to choose from in their checkout process.

Here we apply the name of our shipping method within our bare-bones template. For the sake of demonstration, we'll call ours BareBonesMethod in the code to follow.

Our adaptor in this case will be placed in:/app/code/local/MagentoBook/ ShippingModule/Model/Carrier/BareBonesMethod.php

```php
<?php
class MagentoBook_ShippingModule_Model_Carrier_BareBonesMethod extends
    Mage_Shipping_Model_Carrier_Abstract
{
  protected $_code = 'shippingmodule';
```

```
public function collectRates(Mage_Shipping_Model_Rate_Request
  $request)
{
  if (!$this->getConfigData('active')) {
    Mage::log('The '.$this->_code.' shipping method is not
      active.');
    return false;
  }

  $handling = $this->getConfigData('handling');

  $result = Mage::getModel('shipping/rate_result');

  foreach ($response as $method) {
    $rMethod = Mage::getModel('shipping/rate_result_method');

    $method->setCarrier($this->_code);
    $method->setCarrierTitle($this->getConfigData('title'));

    $method->setMethod($method['code']);
    $method->setMethodTitle($method['title']);

    $method->setCost($method['amount']);

    $method->setPrice($method['amount']+$handling);

    $result->append($method);
  }

  return $result;
  }
}
```

In this example, `$response` is the parsed array of an API call response to a third-party service and `code`, `title`, and `amount` are all values of the array resulting from the request. We'll go through this block by block, so that we're aware of the happenings at each stage:

We start by declaring our module and ensuring that it extends the shipping class of Magento. This tells Magento that the module is a shipping module.

```php
<?php

class MagentoBook_ShippingModule_Model_Carrier_BareBonesMethod extends
    Mage_Shipping_Model_Carrier_Abstract
{
  protected $_code = 'shippingmodule';
```

We need to declare the standard `collectRates` function for Magento to call, when our shipping method is called.

```php
public function collectRates(Mage_Shipping_Model_Rate_Request
  $request)
  {
```

We'll skip the rest if our module isn't enabled and log it to the Magento logs, so that we know it is being skipped.

```php
    if (!$this->getConfigData('active')) {
      Mage::log('The '.$this->_code.' shipping method is not
active.');
      return false;
    }
```

We want to retrieve our configured handling fee to be added later to the total fee for this shipping method.

```php
$handling = $this->getConfigData('handling');
```

We grab our overall result that is being returned to Magento, with all available shipping modules and rates. We do that in case we need to add to it with any methods available with our module.

```php
$result = Mage::getModel('shipping/rate_result');
```

`$response` in the code below is a theoretical example that we have returning from a third-party API, likely via SOAP or another method. This is not a set array here, but used as an example for adding multiple rates based on an array.

```php
foreach ($response as $method) {
```

We prepare the new method that will be added.

```php
$method = Mage::getModel('shipping/rate_result_method');
```

Next, we record our important internal system variables that Magento will use to store and refer to this shipping method.

```
$method->setCarrier($this->_code);
$method->setCarrierTitle($this->getConfigData('title'));
```

Moving on, we add the method's code and title returned in our array to the new shipping method which will be returned to the user.

```
$method->setMethod($method['code']);
$method->setMethodTitle($method['title']);
```

We set the cost, again from the returned array we have. This is not returned to the user, but is used internally by the system to calculate profit (price – cost = profit).

```
$method->setCost($method['amount']);
```

We set the price for the shipping method and add our handling fee that we gathered earlier from the configured administration value.

```
$method->setPrice($method['amount']+$handling);
```

Next, we add the rate to the result which will be returned to the system.

```
    $result->append($method);
}
```

The result is returned to Magento for continuing processing onto the next shipping module installed in the system.

```
    return $result;
  }
}
```

The administration setup

Now that we have an adaptor, we need to make it configurable within the system. We must do so for the Magento administrator to be able to do something constructive with what we've built. The administrator must be able to:

- Enter personal details
- Set up the handling rate
- Set the cost of the shipping method that we put into the store

Our administration configuration file defines how our shipping module appears within the system configuration; which fields appear and what they relate to are defined here. Once defined, the Magento administrator is able to configure the module using these fields to get the desired result from the shipping module.

The file /app/code/local/MagentoBook/ShippingModule/etc/system.xml file contains all the administration fields for the shipping method, and will be formatted along the lines of the following code:

```xml
<?xml version="1.0"?>
<config>
  <sections>
    <carriers>
      <groups>
        <shippingmodule translate="label" module="shipping">
          <label>Bare Bones Shipping inc.</label>
          <frontend_type>text</frontend_type>
          <sort_order>13</sort_order>
          <show_in_default>1</show_in_default>
          <show_in_website>1</show_in_website>
          <show_in_store>1</show_in_sto        <fields>
            <active translate="label">
                <label>Enabled</label>
                <frontend_type>select</frontend_type>
<source_model>adminhtml/system_config_source_yesno</source_model>
                <sort_order>1</sort_order>
                <show_in_default>1</show_in_default>
                <show_in_website>1</show_in_website>
                <show_in_store>1</show_in_store>
            </active>
            <contentdesc translate="label">
                <label>Package Description</label>
                <frontend_type>text</frontend_type>
                <sort_order>12</sort_order>
                <show_in_default>1</show_in_default>
                <show_in_website>1</show_in_website>
                <show_in_store>1</show_in_store>
            </contentdesc>
            {specific configurable fields listed here}
          </fields>
        </shippingmodule>
      </groups>
    </carriers>
  </sections>
</config>
```

In this configuration file, we've simply set the options for whether or not the shipping method is enabled and for a field to describe the contents of our shipping method to the user checking out through the Magento checkout process. We will learn how these fields are formatted, so that we can add our own as we want. We will go through this in the next section.

Declaring further fields and learning how they're structured

A large number of fields are not included in system.xml, as they can be overwhelming without a thorough explanation. We'll pick and choose our fields from the below code and insert them between the `<fields>` `</fields>` tag as we go through the popular types of fields which can be used for the configuration of our module. Our fields are all built up in the same format, with the required options for each field being set out in the format below:

```
<account translate="label">
<label>Account number</label>
<frontend_type>text</frontend_type>
<sort_order>7</sort_order>
<show_in_default>1</show_in_default>
<show_in_website>1</show_in_website>
<show_in_store>1</show_in_store>
</account>
```

Breaking it down, we start with the surrounding tags of `<account translate="label">` `</account>`, which defines the configurable variable `account` and contains its configuration. The `translate="label"` is a reference to the `<translate>` tag that we defined earlier for translation of our module (for multi-language stores). The value inside the tag will act as a key in the language file when translating.

The `<label>` `</label>` tag pair contains the name of this configurable variable to be displayed within the administration. We try to make this short in most cases, with additional notes added where they are needed.

The `<frontend_type>` `</frontend_type>` tag pair defines the type of field that will be shown on the frontend for the administrator configuring this shipping method. This should be set to one of the following:

- text—For a text-input-based form element
- select—For a select-dropdown form element
- multiselect—For allowing the user to select multiple options from a list
- textarea—For a textarea-input-based form element

`<sort_order> </sort_order>` defines the order of the fields when they are output within the administration for the shipping method.

The final three variables for each field (that need to be defined) decide when the configurable variable should appear within the administration. Their values are always 1 or 0 to define yes or no. Here is a breakdown of the individual tags that explains to us what they do:

Tag pair	What they do
`<show_in_default> </show_in_default>`	Default Magento-wide configuration
`<show_in_website> </show_in_website>`	Website-wide configuration
`<show_in_store> </show_in_store>`	Store-specific configuration

There is one additional option tag that is not required, but is important for certain types of fields. The `<source_model> </source_model>` tag pair defines a source model which will populate options for a field. We consider the following as an example of this:

```
<active translate="label">
  <label>Enabled</label>
  <frontend_type>select</frontend_type>
  <source_model>adminhtml/system_config_source_yesno</source_model>
  <sort_order>1</sort_order>
  <show_in_default>1</show_in_default>
  <show_in_website>1</show_in_website>
  <show_in_store>1</show_in_store>
</active>
```

This particular source model `adminhtml/system_config_source_yesno` populates the select field with yes and no options for selection. The raw models for exploration of all the available included functions for the value of this option within your field can be found in: `/app/code/core/Mage/Adminhtml/Model/System/Config/Source/`.

For our `adminhtml/system_config_source_yesno` value, the file in question is `Yesno.php` within the same directory.

Here are a few more source models and what they produce in our module's administration for the user:

- `shipping/source_handlingType` — Lists Magento handling types for shipping modules
- `shipping/source_handlingAction` — Lists Magento handling actions for shipping modules

- `adminhtml/system_config_source_shipping_allspecificcountries` — Prints out a list containing the two core options All allowed countries and Specific countries

- `adminhtml/system_config_source_country` — Lists all countries in the system. It is usually used by means of multi-select lists for shipping modules and payment gateways to select the country that they should be applicable to

Appearing in the administration

Once this has been done, the shipping method should appear in **Shipping Methods** under **System->Configuration**:

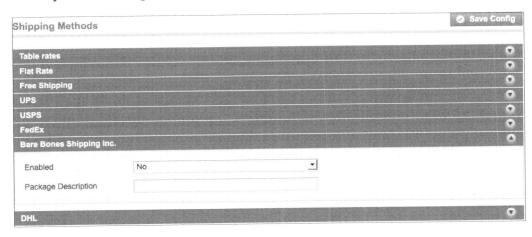

Now, we will look at the most useful shipping module fields that are used when putting the shipping module together. These are fields with predefined names and types that have automatically processed the results that they output. Therefore, they require no additional coding in the adaptor module to take them on board; Magento performs these methods straight out of the box.

Free shipping

If we want to enable an automatic price-based amount for free shipping with our method, we can add in a field called `free_shipping_enable` and combine this with another field by the name of `free_shipping_subtotal`. When `free_shipping_enable` is set to **Enabled** by the Magento administrator, then Magento will automatically take `free_shipping_subtotal` into account and offer free shipping if the total amount is above the value of `free_shipping_subtotal`.

If this field is disabled, Magento will simply process using the default shipping calculation behavior of the module.

The fields are set up as follows, with `sort_order` and `show_in_` values varying:

```
<free_shipping_enable translate="label">
    <label>Free shipping with minimum order amount</label>
    <frontend_type>select</frontend_type>
    <source_model>adminhtml/system_config_source_enabledisable</
source_model>
    <sort_order>21</sort_order>
    <show_in_default>1</show_in_default>
    <show_in_website>1</show_in_website>
    <show_in_store>1</show_in_store>
</free_shipping_enable>
<free_shipping_subtotal translate="label">
    <label>Minimum order amount for free shipping</label>
    <frontend_type>text</frontend_type>
    <sort_order>22</sort_order>
    <show_in_default>1</show_in_default>
    <show_in_website>1</show_in_website>
    <show_in_store>1</show_in_store>
</free_shipping_subtotal>
```

Handling

Handling charges sometimes come into the equation and need to be added onto the overall transaction. Magento enables us to do this using the following source models to present what we want to achieve:

```
<handling_type translate="label">
  <label>Calculate Handling Fee</label>
  <frontend_type>select</frontend_type>
  <source_model>shipping/source_handlingType</source_model>
  <sort_order>10</sort_order>
  <show_in_default>1</show_in_default>
  <show_in_website>1</show_in_website>
  <show_in_store>0</show_in_store>
</handling_type>
<handling_action translate="label">
  <label>Handling Applied</label>
  <frontend_type>select</frontend_type>
  <source_model>shipping/source_handlingAction</source_model>
  <sort_order>11</sort_order>
  <show_in_default>1</show_in_default>
  <show_in_website>1</show_in_website>
  <show_in_store>0</show_in_store>
</handling_action>
```

```
<handling_fee translate="label">
  <label>Handling fee</label>
  <frontend_type>text</frontend_type>
  <sort_order>12</sort_order>
  <show_in_default>1</show_in_default>
  <show_in_website>1</show_in_website>
  <show_in_store>1</show_in_store>
</handling_fee>
```

Restricting a shipping method to certain countries

This will allow us to present the option to the administrator for filtering the shipping method to be only accessible to certain countries. In practice, this means that if we wanted to offer only one type of delivery to the United Kingdom, then we could do so simply by selecting United Kingdom from the multi-select field created by the following declaration.

The Magento administrator can choose the specific countries from the multiple select list. Only orders from those countries that we have created shipping methods for will be processed in the shipping module. This enables them to choose any number of countries for restricting this shipping method to.

```
<sallowspecific translate="label">
  <label>Ship to applicable countries</label>
  <frontend_type>select</frontend_type>
  <sort_order>90</sort_order>
  <frontend_class>shipping-applicable-country</frontend_class>
<source_model>adminhtml/system_config_source_shipping_
allspecificcountries</source_model>
  <show_in_default>1</show_in_default>
  <show_in_website>1</show_in_website>
  <show_in_store>1</show_in_store>
</sallowspecific>
<specificcountry translate="label">
  <label>Ship to Specific countries</label>
  <frontend_type>multiselect</frontend_type>
  <sort_order>91</sort_order>
<source_model>adminhtml/system_config_source_country</source_model>
  <show_in_default>1</show_in_default>
  <show_in_website>1</show_in_website>
  <show_in_store>1</show_in_store>
</specificcountry>
<showmethod translate="label">
  <label>Show method if not applicable</label>
  <frontend_type>select</frontend_type>
```

```
            <sort_order>92</sort_order>
        <source_model>adminhtml/system_config_source_yesno</source_model>
            <show_in_default>1</show_in_default>
            <show_in_website>1</show_in_website>
            <show_in_store>1</show_in_store>
        </showmethod>
```

Using our template to create a shipping method

Now that we have our bare-bones shipping module, we continue with the creation of something that we can see an outcome from. From this we should be able to start to put together our own shipping module tailor-made for future needs.

The purpose of what we are going to build is going to be very simple: we're going to create a shipping module that meets the following parameters:

- It has a handling fee, either per product or for the entire order
- It can be limited to specific countries
- It can set a simple flat-rate shipping cost, if 10 products or more are being ordered
- It can set another simple flat-rate shipping cost, if 10 products or less are being ordered
- All of the above can be configured via the Magento administration

Before progressing, we delete the previous shipping module from our installation to make sure that it does not interfere with what we'll be building. To do this, we go back to the Magento Downloader (which we've learned about in Chapter 2) and select **Uninstall** from the module's supporting dropdown before committing the changes.

The configuration files

This time, we'll go with the directory `MagentoBook` and the name `FullShippingModule`. For this, our `/app/code/local/MagentoBook/ShippingModule/MagentoBook/FullShippingModule/etc/config.xml` file will look like:

```
<?xml version="1.0"?>
<config>
  <modules>
    <MagentoBook_FullShippingModule>
```

```
          <version>0.1.0</version>
          <depends>
            <Mage_Shipping />
          </depends>
        </MagentoBook_FullShippingModule>
      </modules>

      <global>
        <models>
          <FullShippingModule>
          <class>MagentoBook_FullShippingModule_Model</class>
          </FullShippingModule>
        </models>

        <resources>
          <fullshippingmodule_setup>
            <setup>
              <module>MagentoBook_FullShippingModule</module>
            </setup>
            <connection>
              <use>core_setup</use>
              </connection>
          </fullshippingmodule_setup>
        </resources>
      </global>
    </config>
```

We turn on FullShippingModule, and allow it to be turned off/on from within the administration. Then, we create /app/etc/modules/MagentoBook_ FullShippingModule.xml and place the following in it:

```
<?xml version="1.0"?>
<config>
  <modules>
    <MagentoBook_FullShippingModule>
      <active>true</active>
      <codePool>local</codePool>
    </MagentoBook_FullShippingModule>
  </modules>
</config>
```

Our adaptor

For those interested in cutting down on code, unnecessary comments have been removed (which were included in the previous adaptor in this chapter).

We place the following code in: `/app/code/local/MagentoBook/`
`FullShippingModule/Model/Carrier/FullBoneMethod.php`

```php
<?php

class MagentoBook_FullShippingModule_Model_Carrier_FullBoneMethod
extends Mage_Shipping_Model_Carrier_Abstract
{
  protected $_code = 'fullshippingmodule';

  public function collectRates(Mage_Shipping_Model_Rate_Request
    $request)
  {
    if (!$this->getConfigData('active')) {
      Mage::log('The '.$this->_code.' shipping method is not
      active.');
      return false;
    }

    $handling = $this->getConfigData('handling');

    $result = Mage::getModel('shipping/rate_result');
    $method = Mage::getModel('shipping/rate_result_method');
    $items = Mage::getModel('checkout/session')->getQuote()-
                >getAllItems();

    if (count($items) >= $this->getConfigData('minimum_item_limit')) {
      $code = $this->getConfigData('over_minimum_code');
      $title = $this->getConfigData('over_minimum_title');
      $price = $this->getConfigData('over_minimum_price');
    }
    else {
      $code = $this->getConfigData('under_minimum_code');
      $title = $this->getConfigData('under_minimum_title');
      $price = $this->getConfigData('under_minimum_price');
    }

    $method->setCarrier($this->_code);
    $method->setCarrierTitle($this->getConfigData('title'));
    $method->setMethod($code);
```

```
$method->setMethodTitle($title);
$method->setPrice($price + $handling);
$result->append($method);

return $result;
    }
}
```

In short, this will check whether there are more items in the cart than the pre-configured value of `minimum_item_limit` and then apply a rate if it is over the set limit. If under the limit, it applies another rate.

We'll go through the code in blocks, so that we can understand it better.

First we declare our module as an extended class of `Mage_Shipping`, to make sure Magento knows it as a shipping method.

```php
<?php

class MagentoBook_FullShippingModule_Model_Carrier_FullBoneMethod
extends Mage_Shipping_Model_Carrier_Abstract
{
   protected $_code = 'fullshippingmodule';
```

We declare our `collectRates` function, which is the standard function for Magento to call with the request for rates when processing through all available shipping methods to it when a user is at the shipping method stage of ordering.

```
   public function collectRates(Mage_Shipping_Model_Rate_Request
$request)
     {
```

Here we'll use an active variable set in the backend, when the administrator wants to disable this shipping method. We will check if the active variable is set to true and if it is not, false will be returned, so that Magento does not process any further. We will then tell the module to write to Magento's debug log using the `Mage::log` function call to ensure that we're aware the module isn't being used when going through them at any point in our development process.

```
     if (!$this->getConfigData('active')) {
       Mage::log('The '.$this->_code.' shipping method is not
                 active.');
       return false;
     }
```

We get our handling fee configuration value for adding onto our shipping method price later on. This variable has been set in the administration of our module and we're getting it out of the database to be used dynamically.

```
$handling = $this->getConfigData('handling');
```

We make sure that our shipping method is declared to the system and that the result array is sent to the user of shipping methods, if we want to add any available methods.

In practice this means that we set our method (if available), then add this method to the result. The result in total (after going through all shipping modules installed in the system) is then returned to the user for selection of the preferred shipping method.

We also want to get the total amount of items in the cart, as our module depends on it.

```
$result = Mage::getModel('shipping/rate_result');
$method = Mage::getModel('shipping/rate_result_method');
$items = Mage::getModel('checkout/session')->getQuote()
                                        ->getAllItems();
```

If the amount of items in the current order is more than or equal to the amount that the `minimum_item_limit` variable is set to, we want discounted rates. Otherwise, we get the standard rates, as there is no discount.

```
if (count($items) >= $this->getConfigData('minimum_item_limit')) {
  $code = $this->getConfigData('over_minimum_code');
  $title = $this->getConfigData('over_minimum_title');
  $price = $this->getConfigData('over_minimum_price');
}
else {
  $code = $this->getConfigData('under_minimum_code');
  $title = $this->getConfigData('under_minimum_title');
  $price = $this->getConfigData('under_minimum_price');
}
```

We now need to set the internal code Magento will refer to this shipping method as when setting up orders and invoices in the system. We will then set its title and price to also be presented in the system and to the user on the frontend who is awaiting presentation of available shipping methods to them.

```
$method->setCarrier($this->_code);
$method->setCarrierTitle($this->getConfigData('title'));
$method->setMethod($code);
$method->setMethodTitle($title);
$method->setPrice($price + $handling);
```

```
    $result->append($method);

    return $result;
  }
}
```

The administration configuration

First, we'll create the `/app/code/local/MagentoBook/FullShippingModule/etc/system.xml` file using the bare-bones template we put together earlier in this chapter. We start by changing our carrier label to **Full Boned Shipping inc**.

```
<fullshippingmodule translate="label" module="shipping">
  <label>Full Boned Shipping inc.</label>
```

Then we add our text-based fields to the `system.xml` configuration file, `front_end_type` text as per the previous conventions that we used with the following labels and variable names:

Variable Name	Label
minimum_item_limit	**Minimum item quantity** (if over, the over minimum rate is applied)
over_minimum_code	**Over minimum shipping code**
over_minimum_title	**Over minimum title**
over_minimum_price	**Over minimum price**
under_minimum_code	**Under minimum shipping code**
under_minimum_title	**Under minimum title**
under_minimum_price	**Under minimum price**

Here's a reminder of the format for the field tags and how they should be formatted:

```
<active translate="label">
  <label>Enabled</label>
  <frontend_type>select</frontend_type>
  <source_model>adminhtml/system_config_source_yesno</source_model>
  <sort_order>1</sort_order>
  <show_in_default>1</show_in_default>
  <show_in_website>1</show_in_website>
  <show_in_store>1</show_in_store>
</active>
```

We make sure to define our sort order as we proceed. As a reminder—the `<sort_order>1</sort_order>` tag pair is how the order in which the fields appear is controlled. From 1 being the field to appear first, the highest number appears last in sequence.

After we have defined these fields, we add the handling fields and country restriction fields (outlined previously in this chapter). Once this is done, we have completed our configuration.

Testing our newly built module

We go into the administration under **System->Configuration** and then to **Shipping Methods**. Our new shipping method **Full Boned Shipping inc.** appears at the bottom.

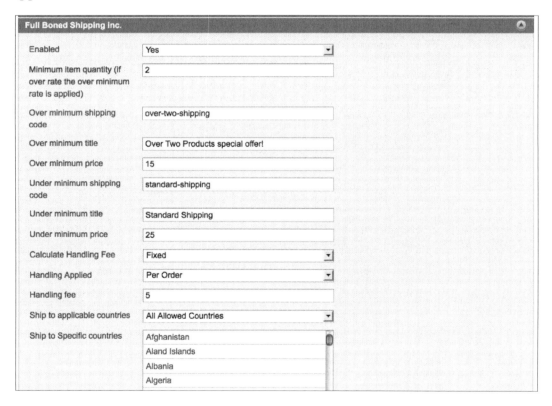

We must be sure to fill out the values here in the module and save them. In the previous screenshot, we have a **Standard Shipping** method, as there are less than two products in the cart. It provides **Over Two Products special offer!** shipping option when the user has equal to or over that amount of products in their cart. The pricing of both options has been set to reflect that and a handling charge of 5 per order has been added, which is applied as per the base currency (Pounds in this case).

To test the frontend, we go to the store and place x amount of products into the cart (either below or above the minimum item quantity set in our module) and progress to shipping to check if the rates are output. If we see them, then it works successfully!

Code to allow our shipping module to meet our needs

Here we see some small pieces of code to use within our shipping modules to achieve what we set out to do, when we created the module for a Magento store.

To get all items in the cart, we use:

```
$items = Mage::getModel('checkout/session')->getQuote()-
>getAllItems();
foreach($items as $item) {
  // process each item here
};
```

Within the items `foreach` loop, we get the quantity for each item that is currently in the cart (also a great way to advance the `fullbonesmodule` built above):

```
$item_quantity = $item->getQty();
```

We check if a product is virtual or not, so that we don't need to calculate shipping:

```
if($item->getProduct()->getTypeInstance()->isVirtual()){
  // it's a virtual product
} else{
  // it's not a virtual product
}
```

Summary

In this chapter we've learned:

- How to set up a basic bare-bones shipping module template for use in the future development of shipping modules

- How to use shipping module-specific fields to limit our shipping module usage to certain countries

- How to set up a basic administration section for our shipping module to allow it to be configured by Magento store administrators

- How to put together a shipping method that decides on the shipping rate by the amount of items in the cart

- Some useful pieces of code to use in our own shipping modules, when putting them together

Further to this chapter, we should create our own shipping modules for Magento stores. It is an excellent opportunity to test the knowledge gained in this chapter, by building modules on our own.

5
Building a Payment Module for Magento

This chapter is about putting together a payment method for Magento and the various aspects that go together to complete the process. We'll be using our knowledge from Chapter 3 on Magento's architecture and grow what we've put into action in Chapter 4 in building our shipping module.

In this chapter we'll go through the various parts that make up a payment method, including:

- The declaration
- The configuration
- The functional operation
- The administrative setup of fields
- Tying in automatic shipping-tracking code generation and updating into our payment module

How payment methods work in Magento

When it comes to going through an order in Magento, payment methods are the last stage of the process. Once customer details have been filled in and the shipping method has been chosen, the payment method comes into play. Its role is to finalize the order and handle how the customer is going to pay for the item(s) that he will be ordering through the Magento installation.

Magento will take all the order details, including what items are in the order, where it is being shipped, and all the pricing totals, after which it will proceed to the payment stage. Magento will load payment methods, one by one and present them to the customer.

Once the customer has selected a payment method, then Magento will progress towards processing through the method's function for sending the data for processing. This could be anything from sending the request via an API, processing credit card details, or authorizing them.

The other functions of a payment method are to handle the invoicing, capturing, voiding, and refunding of payment itself. These are all functions that the payment method will deal, which we'll go through later on in the chapter.

Payment methods that are bundled with Magento

Let's take some time here to go through the existing payment modules that are bundled with Magento by default, so that we may learn from them by exploring their inner depths. It helps a great deal when trying to underneath payment methods to explore the files in these bundled modules and read through the code as best we can, trying to understand how everything works.

There are numerous bundled payment methods included with Magento and they are listed below, with their module names and the subsequent attached payment gateways that they integrate into Magento:

- Amazon Payments (module folder name: AmazonPayments)
- Authorize.Net (module folder name: PayGate)
- Google Checkout (module folder name: GoogleCheckout)
- Magento standard methods: (module folder name: Payment)
    - Cheque/Money order
    - Purchase order
    - Saved CC
    - Zero Subtotal Checkout
- PayPal (module folder names: PayPal, PayPalUk)

Exploring through these bundled payment methods after reading through this chapter will hopefully give us a fuller picture of how they work. A lot can be learnedby jumping into the directories and files of pre-built modules that are out there.

Downloadable payment methods on Magento Connect

In addition to bundled payment methods that come with Magento's default installation, there are well over 100 downloadable extensions on Magento Connect available for download. These vastly cover the majority of popular payment gateways that we would want to implement for our installation, including—but not limited to—the likes of the following:

- 2checkout
- ePay
- Fontis
- Moneybookers
- Sage Pay (formally Protx)
- WorldPay

We'll also find functional non-payment processing methods such as:

- Bank pre-payment
- Cash on delivery

 These modules show only a small piece of what is possible with development of Magento's payment methods and I hope to show you how to get started with building them in this chapter. Many more payment modules can be found online on Magento Connect (http://www.magentocommerce.com/magento-connect) and it is worth browsing through modules under the Payment Gateways filter, with over 200 individual payment modules available. Looking through these modules and downloading some of them will allow you to discover how the internals work as well as what's possible with payment modules.

Let's get started by building a base payment method, which we can build upon and fill in the gaps with to create our desired method.

Building the base of a payment method

Here, we're going to build the base of a payment method. This is something that won't have a purpose, but to provide us with a base—which we can build on—to create our fuller featured payment method.

It will show us what the bare bones are in order for you to be able to later go on and create a fully functional method later on.

Module declaration

We need to start by declaring our module to the system. We'll do this by creating the file `MagentoBook_PaymentModule.xml` in `/app/etc/modules/` and filling it with the following XML code:

```
<?xml version="1.0"?>
<config>
  <modules>
    <MagentoBook_PaymentModule>
      <active>true</active>
      <codePool>local</codePool>
      <depends>
        <Mage_Payment />
      </depends>
      <version>0.1.0</version>
    </MagentoBook_PaymentModule>
  </modules>
</config>
```

A noticeable feature is that we're using the `<depends></depends>` tags, to ensure that this module cannot be activated or used without `Mage_Payment` being activated. This means that if the core payment-handling module in Magento has been disabled, then the module will not be activated or used in any way by the system.

Module configuration

We're now going to move onto the configuration of our module, so that we can fit it into the system and make sure it works with other internal components.

We'll create a file called `config.xml` in `/app/code//MagentoBook/PaymentModule/etc/` and fill it with the following XML code:

```
<?xml version="1.0"?>
<config>
  <modules>
```

```xml
    <MagentoBook_PaymentModule>
      <version>0.1.0</version>
    </MagentoBook_PaymentModule>
  </modules>
  <global>
    <models>
      <paymentmodule>
        <class>MagentoBook_PaymentModule_Model</class>
      </paymentmodule>
    </models>
    <resources>
      <paymentmodule_setup>
        <setup>
          <module>MagentoBook_PaymentModule</module>
        </setup>
        <connection>
          <use>core_setup</use>
        </connection>
      </paymentmodule_setup>
      <paymentmodule_write>
        <connection>
          <use>core_write</use>
        </connection>
      </paymentmodule_write>
      <paymentmodule_read>
        <connection>
          <use>core_read</use>
        </connection>
      </paymentmodule_read>
    </resources>
  </global>
  <default>
    <payment>
      <paymentmodule>
        <active>0</active>
        <model>paymentmodule/paymentMethod</model>
        <order_status>1</order_status>
        <title>Credit Card (Magento Book Payment Module)</title>
        <cctypes>AE,VI,MC,DI</cctypes>
        <payment_action>authorize</payment_action>
      </paymentmodule>
    </payment>
  </default>
</config>
```

Let's back up slightly here and break parts of this configuration down, so that everything is clear before we continue.

We start by defining our XML version and the module version. This version number is used for upgrades of the script later if database upgrades of data stored or table structures are needed as the script progresses over time. In practice, this means that if we need to make changes between versions, we can use Magento's built-in version-control system for modules to deploy scripts between upgrades. This is primarily used for executing changes, such as database structure or changes to the database contents between upgrades. Code-only changes between upgrades should be fine, without an upgrade script attachment to execute any actions:

```xml
<?xml version="1.0"?>
<config>
  <modules>
    <MagentoBook_PaymentModule>
      <version>0.1.0</version>
    </MagentoBook_PaymentModule>
  </modules>
```

We'll now open our `<global></global>` tags for declaration of models and handling of database resources to the system. We'll begin by declaring our model:

```xml
<global>
  <models>
    <paymentmodule>
      <class>MagentoBook_PaymentModule_Model</class>
    </paymentmodule>
  </models>
```

Next, we'll declare our handling of the database resources to the system. Here, we're using `core_setup`, `core_write`, and `core_read` as our declarations because we don't want to use any external database with this module. We would want to simply use the existing Magento database setup:

```xml
<resources>
  <paymentmodule_setup>
    <setup>
      <module>MagentoBook_PaymentModule</module>
    </setup>
    <connection>
      <use>core_setup</use>
    </connection>
  </paymentmodule_setup>
  <paymentmodule_write>
    <connection>
```

```
        <use>core_write</use>
      </connection>
    </paymentmodule_write>
    <paymentmodule_read>
      <connection>
        <use>core_read</use>
      </connection>
    </paymentmodule_read>
  </resources>
</global>
```

Now we'll set up our default configuration for this module and make sure it is under the **payment system** configuration tab in the system. We use the `<payment></payment>` tags here (surrounding this part of the configuration) to declare to Magento that this is a payment module to be added to the system:

```
<default>
  <payment>
    <paymentmodule>
```

We've to make sure that this module isn't set to `active` by default, when it's installed. We'll have to set it to `1` if we want it to automatically become active:

```
<active>0</active>
```

We must ensure that we're referencing the `paymentMethod` model:

```
<model>paymentmodule/paymentMethod</model>
```

We'll set the default order status for new orders to **processing**:

```
<order_status>1</order_status>
```

We'll name our block of configurable variables in the administration:

```
<title>Credit Card (Magento Book Payment Module)</title>
```

Then we'll define which credit card types are available to this module:

```
<cctypes>AE,VI,MC,DI</cctypes>
```

The default payment action for this module is now declared. This is a choice between **Authorize** and **Authorize and Capture**. **Authorize** confirms that the payment method is correct and valid, whereas **Authorize and Capture** grabs the payment from the account at the same time as verification. There are two possible values for this tag: `authorize` and `authorize_capture`. The differences between these two core functions will be explained later in the chapter.

```
<payment_action>authorize</payment_action>
```

We can then close all our open tags to make sure this file is processed properly:

```
        </paymentmodule>
      </payment>
    </default>
  </config>
```

Hopefully this has brought us closer to understanding the payment method's configuration file.

The adaptor model

Our adaptor model is responsible for adapting the model towards a functional tool to be used by the system. In our case all functionality is stored within this file.

We'll create a file called `PaymentMethod.php` in `/app/code/local/CompanyName/NewModule/Model/` and place the following code within it:

```php
<?php
class MagentoBook_PaymentModule_Model_PaymentMethod extends Mage_
Payment_Model_Method_Cc
{
  protected $_code = 'paymentmodule';
  protected $_isGateway = true;
  protected $_canAuthorize = true;
  protected $_canCapture = true;
  protected $_canCapturePartial = false;
  protected $_canRefund = true;
  protected $_canVoid = true;
  protected $_canUseInternal = true;
  protected $_canUseCheckout = true;
  protected $_canUseForMultishipping = true;
  protected $_canSaveCc = false;
  public function authorize(Varien_Object $payment, $amount)
  {
    $data = $payment->getData();
    /*
$data = array(
    store_id,
    customer_payment_id,
    method,
    additional_data,
    po_number,
    cc_type,
    cc_number_enc,
```

```
            cc_last4,
            cc_owner,
            cc_exp_month,
            cc_exp_year,
            cc_number,
            cc_cid,
            cc_ss_issue,
            cc_ss_start_month,
            cc_ss_start_year,
            parent_id,
            amount_ordered,
            base_amount_ordered,
            shipping_amount,
            base_shipping_amount,
            method_instance)
                */
    }
      public function capture(Varien_Object $payment, $amount)
      {
        // Grab stored payment data array for processing
        $paymentData = unserialize($payment->getAdditionalData());
      }
      public function void(Varien_Object $payment)
      {
        // actions when order is voided occur here
      }
      public function refund(Varien_Object $payment, $amount)
      {
        // actions when order is refunded occur here

      }
    }
    ?>
```

Let's go over the meaning of these initial variables' set up in our payment method class before we continue:

`$_isGateway`	Is this a payment gateway? (Uses authorize or capture methods)
`$_canAuthorize`	Can this module authorize? (Is the authorize function available?)
`$_canCapture`	Can this gateway capture payment? (Is the capture function available?)
`$_canCapturePartial`	Can this module partially capture payments?
`$_canRefund`	Can this module refund payments? (Is the refund function available?)
`$_canVoid`	Can this module void payments? (Is the void function available?)
`$_canUseInternal`	Can this payment module appear in the Magento payment modules administration panel?
`$_canUseCheckout`	Can this module show as a method in the Magento checkout?
`$_canUseForMultishipping`	Is this module multi-shipping compatible?
`$_canSaveCc`	Can this module save credit card information for future processing?

What this code does is that it provides a very solid base for building our payment method. Here, we have:

- Our class declaration and initial payment module declaration to Magento
- Our protected variables which define to Magento what the module can and cannot do, so that it automatically restricts how the module operates
- Four functions defining key operations of a payment method:
    - `authorize()`
    - `capture()`
    - `void()`
    - `refund()`

Payment information storage

The $payment model that gets passed to each of the methods in our class is an instance of Mage_Sales_Model_Order_Payment. Every time a payment is processed, the data for that payment is stored in the sales_flat_quote_payment table. There is an additional_data field that our module could use to store values for each transaction.

Four core components

The four core components of a payment module are key operations that can be defined into two blocks, as follows:

- The processing of the payment prior to completing the sale
- After the order has had its payment successfully authorized and captured

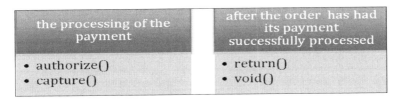

Let's go through both of these now and understand a little more about how the core operations work.

The processing of the payment

The processing of the payment covers the authorize() and capture() functions. Going back to our module's configuration, the <payment_action></payment_action> tags define which of the two functions is called, once the initial order has taken place. We've set this to **Authorize Only**, which by default which will call authorize() and capture() later when we click the capture button after invoicing. But if we choose **Authorize and Capture**, then only the capture() function is called.

Our code for authorizing and capturing payment will need to be placed appropriately within these functions. The choice to be made between the two options should depend on our choice of payment gateway that we're building the module for. An **Authorize Only** approach means that payment is held until we decide to capture it, whereas **Authorize and Capture** will automatically take payment as soon as it is authorized. This will highly depend on the workflow that we had in mind for the module.

Let's recap on how these two functions operate under the two core options in our `<payment_action></payment_action>` tags.

Choice	authorize()	capture()
Authorize Only	Authorizes the customer's payment method via our payment gateway and does not capture the actual payment. It waits for further processing before doing so. This happens when the order is placed and happens automatically.	Once the customer is invoiced via Magento a **capture** button appears in the upper right of the invoice screen within Magento's administration. When clicked, this will then execute the contents of the function for the payment module the user has authorized through. This happens after the order has been placed and it happens manually.
Authorize and Capture	Isn't executed at any point.	Automatically takes care of both the role of `authorize()` and `capture()` functionality at checkout immediately upon the order being placed. Note: This does not call `authorize()` automatically; it will only call `capture()` which should be built to handle both sides of the functionality.

After the order has had its payment successfully processed

The `return()` and `void()` functions are called when an administrator goes into an order after invoicing and clicks the **Return** or **Void** buttons in the upper right of the order screen. The code placed within these functions will determine how the payment method handles an order once these buttons have been clicked.

Declaring configuration options for the admin panel

Now that we have a module with the required functionality and setup, we'll need to declare our configuration options, which appear on the `payment methods` page of the **System -> Configuration** menu.

Setting up the core fields

Create a file called `system.xml` in `/app/code/local/MagentoBook/PaymentModule/etc/` and start by filling it with the following XML code:

```xml
<?xml version="1.0"?>
<config>
  <sections>
    <payment>
      <groups>
        <paymentmodule translate="label" module="paygate">
          <label>NewPayment Module</label>
          <sort_order>670</sort_order>
          <show_in_default>1</show_in_default>
          <show_in_website>1</show_in_website>
          <show_in_store>0</show_in_store>
          <fields>
            {…fields…}
          </fields>
        </paymentmodule>
      </groups>
    </payment>
  </sections>
</config>
```

Replace {…fields…} with the following fieldset XML code:

```xml
<active translate="label">
  <label>Enabled</label>
  <frontend_type>select</frontend_type>
  <source_model>adminhtml/system_config_source_yesno</source_model>
  <sort_order>1</sort_order>
  <show_in_default>1</show_in_default>
  <show_in_website>1</show_in_website>
  <show_in_store>0</show_in_store>
</active>
<order_status translate="label">
  <label>New order status</label>
  <frontend_type>select</frontend_type>
```

```
    <source_model>adminhtml/system_config_source_order_status_processing
    </source_model>
    <sort_order>4</sort_order>
    <show_in_default>1</show_in_default>
    <show_in_website>1</show_in_website>
    <show_in_store>0</show_in_store>
  </order_status>
  <title translate="label">
    <label>Title</label>
    <frontend_type>text</frontend_type>
    <sort_order>2</sort_order>
    <show_in_default>1</show_in_default>
    <show_in_website>1</show_in_website>
    <show_in_store>0</show_in_store>
  </title>
```

As you can see in the XML, it does not matter which order you place the fields in. Only the `sort_order` field name will be used when deciding the order of the fields on output in the section of the Magento administration.

This would create three base fields for the module, as follows:

Field name	What it would be used for
Enabled	To turn the module on/off within the system
New order status	Gives us the ability to choose **Authorize Only** or **Authorize and Capture**
Title	The title of the module when presented to the user

These three fields are a suggested base for the module in order to control the very basics of our payment module. It's a suggestion to enable control of whether or not the module is enabled, the new order status, and the title of the module itself on the frontend when presented to the user as a form of payment method they can choose on checkout.

If we go to **System->Configuration** and choose **Payment Methods** from the sidebar menu, we would see a **New Module** group of configurable options for our module.

Some other field types you can use

There are numerous other fields that we can setup for our module which can be grabbed from pre-existing modules in Magento at the moment. These come in handy as we won't need to set them up ourselves and they slot in easily. A typical field setup is as follows:

```
<title translate="label">
  <label>Title</label>
  <frontend_type>text</frontend_type>
  <sort_order>2</sort_order>
  <show_in_default>1</show_in_default>
  <show_in_website>1</show_in_website>
  <show_in_store>0</show_in_store>
</title>
```

In our scenario the `<frontend_type></frontend_type>` tag pair is the most important tag pair, as this is the only value we change when pre-populating field types. The following are examples of values which can be placed inside these tags to produce different fields:

- `adminhtml/system_config_source_yesno`—returns **yes** or **no** for you field type

- `adminhtml/system_config_source_order_status_new`—returns an array of options for use when selecting a new order's status

- `adminhtml/system_config_source_email_identity`—returns a list of email identities in the system from which to send emails from

- `adminhtml/system_config_source_email_template`—returns a list of email templates in the system from which to send emails with

- `adminhtml/system_config_source_payment_cctype`—returns a list of credit card types, useful for multi-selects when deciding the types of cards that we would want our module to accept

We'll have a look at the file `/app/code/core/Mage/adminhtml/Model/System/Config/Source.php` to see all the options available to us as source models. This could potentially unveil some additional options that will benefit us in our module development.

Obscuring fields

We could use the following pair to obscure data in the backend and reveal the data when it placed back into the field on its way out of the database:

```
<frontend_type>obscure</frontend_type>
<backend_model>adminhtml/system_config_backend_encrypted
</backend_model>
```

This would, of course, be placed within our standard field tag. Take the following example from Google Checkout's setup:

```
<merchant_id translate="label">
  <label>Merchant ID</label>
  <frontend_type>obscure</frontend_type>
  <backend_model>adminhtml/system_config_backend_encrypted
  </backend_model>
  <sort_order>20</sort_order>
  <show_in_default>1</show_in_default>
  <show_in_website>1</show_in_website>
  <show_in_store>0</show_in_store>
</merchant_id>
```

The `backend_model` makes sure it is encrypted when put into the database and the `frontend_type` means that it's unencrypted on the way back out.

Custom fields from our models

We can create our own field population source models by making use of the `Models/` directory. Take the following example from the Google Checkout module's `/app/code/core/Mage/GoogleCheckout/etc/system.xml` file:

```
<checkout_image translate="label">
  <label>Checkout Image Style</label>
  <frontend_type>select</frontend_type>
  <source_model>googlecheckout/source_checkout_image</source_model>
  <sort_order>40</sort_order>
  <show_in_default>1</show_in_default>
  <show_in_website>1</show_in_website>
  <show_in_store>0</show_in_store>
</checkout_image>
```

This calls the model `/app/code/core/Mage/GoogleCheckout/Model/Source/Checkout/Image.php` and the inner function `toOptionArray()`. This returns the values to Magento, which handles the output into the Magento administration. Take a read of the file should you be interested in digging further into how they make it work.

Tying in automatic shipping tracking/updating

The following is an example of payment methods offering a specialized feature in hooking up shipping integration. Hopefully, we should be able to take something from this and be able to either re-apply these methods within our payment modules or apply similar methods in our custom modules built for Magento.

Automatic shippingtracking and code-generation tie-in

Amazon Payments has a setup due to which, if we mark an item as shipped or update the tracking code for that order, then it will report the codes and the status of the order for tracking in their system back to Amazon.

This is useful in several ways:

- It helps the user stay in the loop without coming to the website
- The user somewhat expects this to happen if their payment gateway that they are paying through provides this as functionality with other websites
- This then, of course, helps them relate to our brand more and gives them the unexpected surprise that makes them come back or talk about the site more

This is done via observation on events in the system. The two events that the module observes and then acts upon are:

- The confirmation of an order shipment
- The saving of a tracking shipping number to an order

If the `/app/code/core/Mage/AmazonPayments/etc/config.xml` file is opened in default installation of Magento, we'll see the following code that defines the observers in the system between `<adminhtml></adminhtml>` tags:

```
<events>
  <sales_order_shipment_save_after>
    <observers>
      <amazonpayments>
        <type>model</type>
```

```
          <class>amazonpayments/observer</class>
          <method>confirmShipment</method>
        </amazonpayments>
      </observers>
    </sales_order_shipment_save_after>
    <sales_order_shipment_track_save_after>
      <observers>
        <amazonpayments>
          <type>model</type>
          <class>amazonpayments/observer</class>
          <method>salesOrderShipmentTrackSaveAfter</method>
        </amazonpayments>
      </observers>
    </sales_order_shipment_track_save_after>
  </events>
```

This XML information and set of fields defines the observers so that information is passed to a set type of class and method for processing. Take the second definition for example:

```
<sales_order_shipment_track_save_after>
  <observers>
    <amazonpayments>
      <type>model</type>
      <class>amazonpayments/observer</class>
      <method>salesOrderShipmentTrackSaveAfter</method>
    </amazonpayments>
  </observers>
</sales_order_shipment_track_save_after>
```

This makes sure that when a sales order shipment tracking code is saved, directly afterwards the AmazonPayments module will look for:

- Something in the /model/ folder of (defined in the <type></type> tag pair)
- The AmazonPayments module called Observer.php (defined in the <class></class> tag pair)
- The salesOrderShipmentTrackSaveAfter() method within this file (defined in the <method></method> tag pair)

On the other end of these observers is the model file itself (Observer.php) that sits within the /model/ folder of the AmazonPayments module folder. If we go to /app/code/core/Mage/AmazonPayments/Model/Observer.php we'll see the code for the methods that are on the other end of these observers that are set:

```
class Mage_AmazonPayments_Model_Observer
{
  public function confirmShipment(Varien_Event_Observer $observer)
  {
    $shipment = $observer->getEvent()->getShipment();
    if ($shipment->getOrder()->getPayment()->getMethod() !=
'amazonpayments_cba') {
      return;
    }
    Mage::getModel('amazonpayments/api_cba')
      ->confirmShipment($shipment);
  }
  public function salesOrderShipmentTrackSaveAfter(Varien_Event_
Observer $observer)
  {
    $track = $observer->getEvent()->getTrack();
    $order = $track->getShipment()->getOrder();
    /* @var $order Mage_Sales_Model_Order */
    if ($order->getPayment()->getMethod() != 'amazonpayments_cba') {
      return;
    }
    Mage::getModel('amazonpayments/api_cba')
      ->sendTrackingNumber($order, $track);
  }
}
```

There are a few key areas to pick up upon here that are important when replicating this functionality in your own modules. Let's go through a few certain key blocks to ensure we're benefiting from reading this code.

We start by noticing that Varien_Event_Observer $observer is the only variable being caught within both of these functions. This is how observers are setup and work with the system to properly process the event they are observing. A notable aspect is that these functions are public, and not private.

```
public function confirmShipment(Varien_Event_Observer $observer)
{
```

Next, we've got a block of code for ensuring that the payment method used for this order is actually Amazon Payments CBA. This is important, as Amazon Payments doesn't need to hear about orders placed through other payment gateways. This is vital to ensuring smooth integration of the payment module. If the payment method isn't `amazonpayments_cba` then we can simply return nothing and let Magento carry on as usual through the other observers waiting for this action to occur.

```
$shipment = $observer->getEvent()->getShipment();
if ($shipment->getOrder()->getPayment()->getMethod() !=
'amazonpayments_cba') {
  return;
}
```

It's also important to notice the code separation going on here. The observer class is only used for receiving notification of the event. All actual executed code is in external models that are built for the next step. We can see how they've included an external model here:

```
Mage::getModel('amazonpayments/api_cba')
  ->confirmShipment($shipment);
```

The last thing to notice from the functions at hand is the way they gather the shipping, tracking, and order information and how they make use of the `$observer` class.

```
$shipment = $observer->getEvent()->getShipment();
```

And in the second function within the class:

```
$track = $observer->getEvent()->getTrack();
$order = $track->getShipment()->getOrder();
```

These methods could be used in our observer classes if we wish to place them within our built payment modules.

To see how the objects created by those three functions are processed, open the file `/app/code/core/Mage/AmazonPayments/Model/Api/Cba.php` and search for the functions that the two observer functions execute from this file when looking to the executable action of the observation they were there to observe:

- `confirmShipment`
- `sendTrackingNumber`

These two functions teach us a lot about how to learn more about those three variables created and passed to the functions. They also elaborate on how the three variables are used when passed through to the resulting function.

We'll also see the same two observers across other bundled payment gateways such as Google Checkout, which should be explored for further depth of information on the topic.

Summary

In this chapter, we learned the following:

- Which payment methods are bundled with Magento by default
- The popular payment methods that can be downloaded from Magento Connect
- How to put together the basics of a payment method for Magento and the core functions Magento uses automatically from the methods it uses
- How to setup the fields as well as how to obscure and encrypt them
- How to link in our own pre-populated arrays of field values from our custom models
- Tying in automatic shipping-tracking code generation and updating into our payment module

Further, we should research the other payment methods available on Magento Connect. These will help us learn more about how payment methods are structured and function internally. When we try to create functionality for us, we will learn in depth about the existing payment methods.

We should also be able to create our own payment methods for our Magento installations that need them.

6
Building a Basic Featured
Products Module

In this chapter, we will learn how to put together a basic module in Magento. This module will allow us to feature products on the site and within our product categories. This will introduce us to some of the basics of module development in Magento and enable us to form a fundamental base for future module development.

One of the most implemented features on a Magento site is the ability to feature products. Whether it is the home page, or the sidebar, or the footer, featured products are a fundamental building block of an e-commerce website. Typically this is done through banner advertising, but with this module we'll use the products themselves as a base for our information. We'll display product blocks on the site using this featured product data, gathered dynamically in the administrative backend of Magento.

How it works

To make this happen, we'll set up an attribute in our system to mark a product as featured and then create a bespoke module that will allow us to display products marked as featured on a per category basis.

The process for getting a product to appear in the **Featured Product** block will go as follows:

- Create or edit a product
- Find the field **featured** and select **yes** from the dropdown
- Save the product information that we have changed or created
- Go to a category that this product is assigned to and it will appear

To build our module we will:

- Create the attribute
- Create our module with the core functionality
- Extend the category view to include our featured product display
- Create templates for display
- Define the module in our `local.xml` module configuration file
- Add in our XML block declaration, so that the module displays on the frontend, and get started

Creating the attributes in the system

We'll start by going to **Catalog -> Attributes -> Manage Attributes** from within the administration.

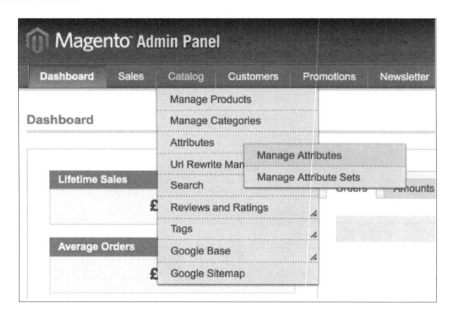

Next, we'll click on **Add New Attribute** in the upper right of the **Manage Attributes** screen.

The **New Product Attribute** screen is shown in the following screenshot:

Setting the field values

We'll set the fields on this page as follows, to set up our **Featured Product** attributes in the system.

Attribute Properties

The properties of each attribute from the previous screenshot is given below:

Field name	Field value
Attribute Code	**featured**
Scope	**Store View**
Catalog Input Type for Store Owner	**Yes/No**
Default Value	**No**
Unique Value (not shared with other products)	**No**
Values Required	**No**
Input Validation for Store Owner	**None**
Apply To	**All Product Types**

Frontend Properties

The **Frontend Properties** are described as follows:

Field name	Field value
Use in quick search	No
Use in advanced search	Yes
Comparable on Front-end	No
Use In Layered Navigation (**it also refers to Multiple Select and Price.**)	No
Visible on Product View Page on Front-end	Yes

 Ignore all other attributes that appear and leave them as their default values

Manage Label/Options

This is found by clicking on the **Manage Label/Options** tab on the left-hand side of the current page.

We chose **Featured Product** as our label for this attribute when displayed. However, we can replace this field value with another one, if we want something else to appear.

Field name	Field value
Admin	**Featured Product**

The **Manage Label/Options** tab will look something like this:

We must remember to save our attribute to complete this section of the chapter.

Following this you will need to go to **Catalog -> Attributes -> Manage Attribute Sets**. Once here select your chosen attribute set that you'd like to add this new featured attribute into. You can repeat this step multiple times, should you want to for each attribute set that you'd like to add the attribute to.

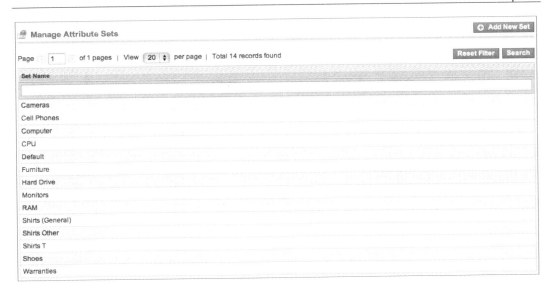

I've chosen to select **Default** in this example.

You should see the attribute that we've created under **Unassigned Attributes** on the right hand side of the screen that now appears.

Proceed by clicking and holding your mouse down to drag and drop the **featured** attribute into the attribute group of your choice in the middle.

You should now see something along the lines of the following with the **featured** attribute under the group:

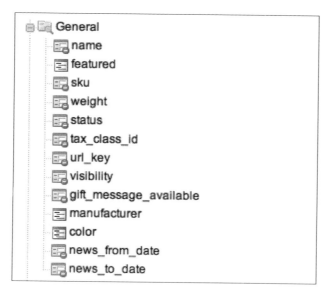

Creating the core module with functionality

We'll now create the function that allows us to present the products that are featured to our block, for displaying them to the end user. The class that we created contains the function that expands existing Magento catalog functionality. This occurs so that we can interact with other catalog functionality directly and integrate directly with the existing class files.

We'll create the file `Featured.php` and the directories to create the path: `app/code/local/MagentoBook/Catalog/Block/Product/Featured.php`.

For adding functionality, we'll edit the newly created `Featured.php` file and place the following in it:

```php
<?php
class MagentoBook_Catalog_Block_Product_Featured extends
                    Mage_Catalog_Block_Product_Abstract
{
  protected $_limit = 1;
  public function getFeaturedProducts()
  {
    $productCollection = Mage::registry('current_category')-
      >getProductCollection();
```

```
    Mage::getModel('catalog/layer')->prepareProductCollection
      ($productCollection);
    $productCollection
      ->addAttributeToFilter('featured', true)
      ->setPageSize($this->_limit)
      ->load();
    return $productCollection;
}
  public function setLimit($limit = null)
  {
    if(intval($limit) > 0)
      $this->_limit = intval($limit);
  }
}
?>
```

Let's break this down, so that we fully understand the contents of the file.

First, we'll declare the class, which will extend the core `Mage_Catalog` module to integrate directly into the system and allow us to interact with core functionality that we need in order to create this module:

```
<?php
class MagentoBook_Catalog_Block_Product_Featured extends
  Mage_Catalog_Block_Product_Abstract
{
```

We'll then set up the `$_limit` variable, which will hold the number of featured products that are to be fetched:

```
protected $_limit = 1;
```

Next, we'll declare `getFeaturedProducts` with which we will grab the featured product for the current category:

```
public function getFeaturedProducts()
    {
```

We'll build `$productCollection` result by building a base line query for **get products for current category**:

```
    $productCollection = Mage::registry('current_category')-
      >getProductCollection();
    Mage::getModel('catalog/layer')->prepareProductCollection
      ($productCollection);
```

We'll then add filters to make sure that we only select where the **Featured** attribute is set to **true** (or **Yes**) and limit the results to the amount stored in the variable (which we set earlier in the class).

```
$productCollection
  ->addAttributeToFilter('featured', true)
  ->setPageSize($this->_limit)
  ->load();
```

This is then returned for usage in the template file of the module's output:

```
    return $productCollection;
}
```

We will end the file with the `setLimit` function, which allows us (or anyone using the module) to override the output limit:

```
public function setLimit($limit = null)
{
  if(intval($limit) > 0)
    $this->_limit = intval($limit);
}
```

We'll end our class declaration and our file:

```
}
?>
```

That completes the class file of our module!

Adding the XML block declaration for display of the module on the frontend

We'll open `/app/design/frontend/default/default/layout/catalog.xml`. We want to add a new `<block>` right above the **Product List** block in the **Default Category** layout.

We'll search for the `<catalog_category_default>` tag and the content within it. Once we've found this, we have two choices as to where we can place our featured content block, The choices are `<reference name="left">` and `<reference name="content">`, which both relate to the left sidebar of our layout and the content layout. We can also add other references between these tags, if the layout requires it.

Once we've chosen the relevant reference tag, we add in the following block to call our module that we have put together every time the category page loads:

```
<block type="catalog/product_featured" name="product_featured"
        as="product_featured"
        template="catalog/product/featured.phtml"></block>
    <block type="catalog/product_featured" name="product_featured"
            template="catalog/product/featured.phtml">
    <action method="setLimit"><limit>2</limit></action>
</block>
```

The template address `catalog/product/featured.phtml`, can be replaced with whatever custom file we want, if we wish to separate the template out from the existing set that comes with Magento's default frontend theme.

It's worth noting that the following code sets how many products should be returned by the template:

```
<action method="setLimit"><limit>2</limit></action>
```

With the code we've just inserted, two featured products will output. To change, simply switch the number '2' for the number of products you'd like to output in your template files.

The `product_featured` return statement from our previous section in putting together the module is featured here. Imagine this block as the part where Magento requests `product_featured` and the `View.php` file that we built above as the part of our module that returns the appropriate content.

Creating templates for display

In order for our module to appear, we need our templates to call the function that we've created at some point. In this case, we presume that we've gone with the choice of `<reference name="content">` and include the featured block in the content area of our layout.

We'll open up the `View.phtml` file located at `/app/design/frontend/default/default/template/catalog/category/View.phtml` and add the following code above the first occurrence of `<?php echo $this->getProductListHtml(); ?>` in this template file:

```
<?php echo $this->getFeaturedProductHtml(); ?>
<?php echo $this->getChildHtml('product_featured'); ?>
```

This will place our **Featured Product** content block above the place where products are output.

We'll now need a physical template file for our featured product block, in order for it to display our featured products. To do this, we'll create `featured.phtml` (if it doesn't exist already) at the location `/app/design/frontend/default/default/template/catalog/product/featured.phtml` and place some code within it to present our featured products out onto the website.

Here is an example that shows (in code order):

- The name of the product linked to its individual product page
- Its image at a 200 x 200 size
- An **Add to Cart** button for the user to add it into their cart directly from where it is displayed
- A check to see if the item is out of stock or not before displaying the **Add to Cart** button, with a warning message if it is in fact out of stock

```php
<?php
foreach($this->getFeaturedProducts() as $_product): ?>
  <form action="<?php echo $this->getAddToCartUrl($_product) ?>"
        method="post" id="product_addtocart_form">
    <a href="<?php echo $_product->getProductUrl() ?>">
      <?php echo $this->htmlEscape($_product->getName()) ?></a>
    <img class="product-image" src="<?php echo
      $this->helper('catalog/image')->init($_product, 'small_image')-
      >resize(200, 200) ?>" alt="<?php echo $this
      ->htmlEscape($_product->getName()) ?>" />
    <?php if($_product
    ->isSaleable()): ?>
      <button class="form-button" onclick="setLocation
        ('<?php echo $this->getAddToCartUrl($_product) ?>')">
        <span><?php echo $this->__('Add to Cart') ?></span></button>
    <?php else: ?>
      <div class="out-of-stock"><?php echo
        $this->__('Out of stock') ?></div>
    <?php endif; ?>
  </form>
<?php endforeach; ?>
```

Defining the module in the local .xml module configuration file

Now that everything is in place, we need to ensure that our module is declared to Magento by including it in our `local.xml` file. We can find this file in the `/app/etc/` directory.

We'll add the following inside the `<config></config>` global tag pair that surrounds all inner declaration tags:

```
<blocks>
  <catalog>
    <rewrite>
      <product_featured>MagentoBook_Catalog_Block_Product_Featured
      </product_featured>
    </rewrite>
    <rewrite>
      <category_view>MagentoBook_Catalog_Block_Category_View
      </category_view>
    </rewrite>
  </catalog>
</blocks>
```

Once this is done, our **Featured Products** module will be included in the system. We do not need to activate/deactivate the module, as it extends a core component of Magento and for this reason does not need to be declared separately.

This concludes adding a featured product section into your Magento category templates.

Summary

In this chapter, we've learned:

- How to put together a basic module in Magento
- How to create a featured product attribute which allows us to feature products by which category the user is currently browsing

We must continue developing these modules further to fit our specific needs, to extend other parts of Magento's core modules, and to integrate what we've learned in this chapter into our Magento implementations.

7
Fully-Featured Module for Magento with Admin Panel

In this chapter, we'll go through the basics of module development, right from getting a simple **Hello World** message displayed to managing the module's information in the database and making it into a dynamic extension of Magento. This extension will be used to manage the output of brands on a page that will be displayed on the frontend of our installation.

We'll go through:

- Getting the module set up using a pre-built module creation tool
- Getting our first **Hello World** displayed on the frontend
- The overall structure of where files should go and what structure to use
- How all the files of the module are put together and what each of them does
- Extending the result into a brand management module
- Displaying the managed results data on the frontend of our Magento installation

We'll start by assembling the basic structure and the files needed to get a Hello World message displayed and proceed ahead to upgrading the module to bring in additional elements. These will include an administration panel and dynamic output to Magento. It will also include giving the module its own unique URL within the installation. It provides our module with a dynamic frontend, using which visitors can browse through the data that is managed in the backend.

Creating our first Hello World message

We'll start with a quick **Hello World** via a display block. This process is more complex than displaying a message directly, but it shows us the fundamentals of what we'll be trying to achieve in this chapter. With the exception of simply typing **Hello World** in an existing template block, this is the quickest way of getting our own template block into Magento's display system.

Setting up the display template

We'll start the process by setting up the template itself with our `Hello world` statement inside of it.

First, we'll create the directory `/app/design/frontend/default/default/template/hello/` and create/place the file `world.phtml` within it. Hence, the full address should be `/app/design/frontend/default/default/template/hello/world.phtml`.

Next, we'll insert our `Hello World` text within the file:

```
<h2>Hello World!</h2>
```

We've placed an `<h2>` tag on either side of the statement so that it stands out on screen.

Placing the display template in a layout .xml file

Now that we have our display template, we need to ensure that the layout block appears on a layout `.xml` file, so that it can be output on the site.

We'll place the following block of code in the layout `.xml` file of our choice:

```
<block type="core/template" name="helloworld" template="hello/world.
phtml" />
```

For example, we'll take the `core.xml` file, which contains the following by default:

```
<?xml version="1.0"?>
<layout version="0.1.0">
    <default>
        <block name="formkey" type="core/template" template="core/
formkey.phtml" />
    </default>
</layout>
```

Let's place our layout block within the XML file and ensure that it appears correctly within the reference name in our layout, in the right-hand column:

```
<?xml version="1.0"?>
<layout version="0.1.0">
    <default>
        <block name="formkey" type="core/template" template="core/
formkey.phtml" />
        <reference name="right">
            <block type="core/template" name="helloworld" template="hello/
world.phtml" />
        </reference>
    </default>
</layout>
```

After we've saved these files, our **Hello world!** message will be displayed in the right sidebar, as shown below:

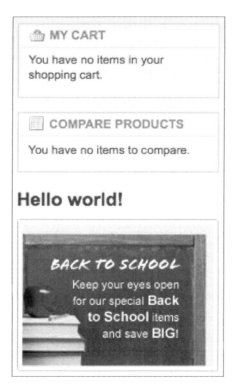

As we can see, the **Hello world!** message is displayed between **Compare Products** and **BACK TO SCHOOL** advertisement.

Creating our first /helloworld/ URL structure

Another step into Magento module development is to create a complete module that becomes a section of the site via having a URL of its own. We're now going to create one of these modules to get ourselves a `/helloworld/` URL structure and a section of the site dedicated to our created module.

First, we need to put together the module's structure before adding the URL. This is so that we're set-up going forward. Should you want to just have the URL for your module, you only need to follow the last step of this section in the chapter.

The directory structure

We'll create and set up folders to match the following directory structure in preparation for putting together the module for the rest of this chapter.

The directories for the module's core files need to be set as follows:

- `/app/code/local/Book/Helloworld/`
    - `Block/`
    - `controllers/`
    - `etc/`
    - `Helper/`
    - `Model/`
    - `Mysql4/`
    - `Helloworld/`
    - `sql/`
    - `helloworld_setup/`

For the module's design template files:

- `/app/design/frontend/default/default/`
    - `template/`
    - `helloworld/`

Giving the module a backend

Now that we have our directory structure in place, we'll need to create a configuration file which makes sure that Magento can view our module in the system.

The file `/app/etc/modules/Book_Helloworld.xml` should be created for our module and should contain the following:

```xml
<?xml version="1.0"?>
<config>
  <modules>
    <Book_Helloworld>
      <active>true</active>
      <codePool>local</codePool>
    </Book_Helloworld>
  </modules>
</config>
```

The module will now appear in the **Disable Modules Output** section under **System->Configuration**, then **Advanced** under the left sub-menu. We can either disable or enable this module through this menu.

 Note: If the module does not appear on the page, then we'll need to clear the Magento installation's cache. To do this, we should go to **System->Cache Management** in our backend menu, select **Disable** from the drop-down to the right of **All Cache**, and click **Save cache settings**.

Configuring the module

Every module requires a `config.xml` file to set it up. In this case, we'll set up a very basic version of the file (and nothing more) to get the module up and running. Later on this file becomes very important in making the module dynamic and we'll extend it much further than this base.

We'll create the file `/app/code/local/Book/Helloworld/etc/config.xml` and fill it with the following:

```xml
<?xml version="1.0"?>
<config>
  <modules>
    <Book_Helloworld>
      <version>0.1.0</version>
    </Book_Helloworld>
  </modules>
  <frontend>
```

```xml
    <routers>
      <helloworld>
        <use>standard</use>
          <args>
          •   <module>Book_Helloworld</module>
              <frontName>helloworld</frontName>
          </args>
      </helloworld>
    </routers>
    <layout>
      <updates>
        <helloworld>
          <file>helloworld.xml</file>
        </helloworld>
      </updates>
    </layout>
  </frontend>
  <global>
    <blocks>
      <helloworld>
        <class>Book_Helloworld_Block</class>
      </helloworld>
    </blocks>
    <helpers>
      <helloworld>
        <class>Book_Helloworld_Helper</class>
      </helloworld>
    </helpers>
  </global>
</config>
```

We'll break the code down and go through each tag individually.

We'll start by defining the `<config>` tag and the XML header for the file:

```xml
<?xml version="1.0"?>
<config>
```

We'll follow it up with the declaration of our module and defining our module version number:

```xml
<modules>
    <Book_Helloworld>
      <version>0.1.0</version>
    </Book_Helloworld>
</modules>
```

Opening the `<frontend>` tag, here we'll be setting up the module's URL; the `<frontName>` tag defines the URL, via which the module will be directly accessed. In our example, we've used `helloworld`, as we want to achieve a `/helloworld/` setup.

```
<frontend>
  <routers>
    <helloworld>
      <use>standard</use>
      <args>
        <module>Book_Helloworld</module>
        <frontName>helloworld</frontName>
      </args>
    </helloworld>
  </routers>
```

We'll continue inside the `<frontend>` tag to define the layout `.xml` file attached to this module. These are the XML blocks that will be processed once the module is accessed directly via the `frontName` value we set in the tag above. In this case, when `/helloworld/` is accessed by a user, the layout `.xml` file will be accessed to get module-specific blocks to load. This is followed by the closing of the `<frontend>` tag, as it concludes our module's frontend configuration tags.

```
<layout>
  <updates>
    <helloworld>
      <file>helloworld.xml</file>
    </helloworld>
  </updates>
</layout>
</frontend>
```

The module's display block models are next. Here, we're declaring that this module has a display block model class, which lets us use this model as display block types in Magento's `.xml` layout files.

```
<global>
  <blocks>
    <helloworld>
      <class>Book_Helloworld_Block</class>
    </helloworld>
  </blocks>
```

Continuing with the `<global>` tag, we'll define our `Helper` model for the module, so that it is available to the blocks when they are used. This is then followed by the closing of the module's `<global>` tag:

```
<helpers>
  <helloworld>
    <class>Book_Helloworld_Helper</class>
  </helloworld>
</helpers>
</global>
```

We'll close the `<config>` tag to end the file and that finishes everything:

```
</config>
```

We now have a `config.xml` file for our module.

Our controller

The module's controller will take in the direct URL and process the layout attached to it. Later on it will be responsible for loading the data to the index of our module, when accessed via `/helloworld/`. At the moment however, it will load just the `<default>` tag from our layout. `.xml` file (which we'll set up later).

We'll create the file `/app/code/local/Book/Helloworld/controllers/IndexController.php` and fill it with the following:

```php
<?php
class Book_Helloworld_IndexController extends Mage_Core_Controller_Front_Action
{
  public function indexAction()
  {
    $this->loadLayout();
    $this->renderLayout();
  }
}
```

There are two core functions to this controller: the first loads the module's layout `.xml` file and processes it:

```
$this->loadLayout();
```

The second function renders this layout using the blocks defined in the layout `.xml` file and outputs it:

```
$this->renderLayout();
```

The Helper model

Not every module uses a Helper model, but we'll be working on one anyway (for illustrating this chapter). We'll be learning about the best practices for using them in our module. Typically, a Helper model will be utilized for its helper functions, which are used for formatting or altering output in some way. Examples of that are as follows:

- Number formatting (currency, number rounding into thousands)
- Alternative row color/class outputting

We'll create the file `/app/code/local/Book/Helloworld/Helper/Data.php` and place the following code within it:

```php
<?php

class Book_Helloworld_Helper_Data extends Mage_Core_Helper_Abstract
{
}
```

At the moment the file is empty in order to set it up for later editing. We will place a function or two in the Helper model later for usage.

The module's default model

All modules have a default model that is attached to them. The default model is responsible for fetching the data and/or setting it up for the module's design template files to process through. It is called when we declare a block, for example **type=hello/world** on a display block would call the `world` function inside the `Hello` model.

We'll create the file `/app/code/local/Book/Helloworld/Model/Helloworld.php` and place the following code within it:

```php
<?php

class Book_Helloworld_Model_Helloworld extends Mage_Core_Model_
Abstract
{
  public function _construct()
  {
    parent::_construct();
    $this->_init('helloworld/helloworld');
  }
}
```

This sets up the model for the module and initializes the model's functions for usage in any template .xml file once we have some blocks.

Template blocks and display

Now we'll need to create the frontend for our module and make sure that Magento has something to output, when our module's chosen URL /helloworld/ is accessed by a user.

Display block class

This holds the functions for the display block to refer to and is needed for our template .xml file to pass the messages across.

We'll create the file /app/code/local/Book/Helloworld/Block/Helloworld.php and place within it the following:

```php
<?php
class Book_Helloworld_Block_Helloworld extends Mage_Core_Block_
Template
{
  public function _prepareLayout()
  {
    return parent::_prepareLayout();
  }
  public function getHelloworld()
  {
    return 'Hello world';
  }
}
```

We can see that we have a getHelloworld function, which will return the **Hello world!** message to our template file.

The layout .xml file

Our module needs a dedicated layout .xml file, in order to load the display blocks for our module when it is accessed.

For that, we'll create the file /app/design/frontend/default/default/layout/helloworld.xml and place the following within it:

```xml
<?xml version="1.0"?>
<layout version="0.1.0">
  <helloworld_index_index>
    <reference name="content">
      <block type="helloworld/helloworld" name="helloworld"
        template="helloworld/helloworld.phtml" />
```

```
        </reference>
      </helloworld_index_index>
    </layout>
```

The design template file

Finally, we have our design template file which will be used for formatting the output from the display block model.

We'll create `/app/design/frontend/default/default/template/Helloworld/helloworld.phtml` and place the following inside it:

```
<h2><?php echo $this->getHelloworld(); ?></h2>
```

This will return the `getHelloWorld()` function from our display block between a pair of `<h2>` tags.

Viewing /helloworld/

Now that we've put everything together that's required, we have our first display block powered **Hello World!**. Accessing `/helloworld/` displays something along the lines of the following, depending on our theme:

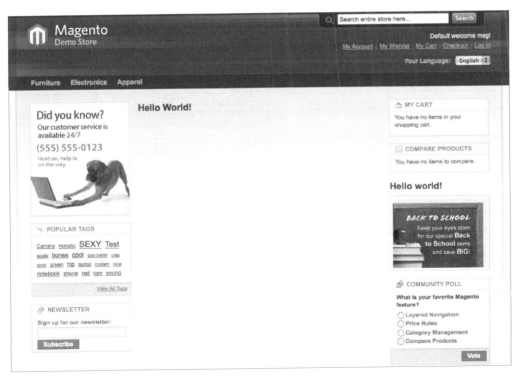

Taking a look at what we've put together

Let's go over all the work that we've just done to create this module and get to this point.

We have created:

- A directory system that holds our module and all its files
- A system configuration file to declare our module to the system
- A module configuration file to declare our module's configuration
- A controller which processes the request when the user loads /helloworld/
- A default model
- A helper for functions to help out with formatting in display templates
- A display block for passing the message to our template file
- A template file for echoing out our **Hello world!** message
- A layout .xml file dedicated to just this module's display blocks under the URL /helloworld/

Using the Module Creator script to get Hello World

We'll now go through an automated method of creating a module with backend administration. This will show us how to quickly deploy a base of a fully featured module in the future. After doing that, we'll go through this code to understand how it all works individually.

We can find the Module Creator available as an extension on Magento Connect at the following link: http://www.magentocommerce.com/extension/1108/modulecreator. Credit for the Module Creator script goes to Daniel Nitz, with the example templates being created by Alistek.

This script allows us to put together a solid base of required files for our modules, without having to manually create each file. It saves some time when creating all the individual files and all developers should know about this when getting into regular module development for Magento. While it's not a substitute for knowing how to put together the modules ourselves, it does help when we need to get a module up and running quickly (most useful when we need a base with which to expand into what we want to build).

Installing the Module Creator

The following sequence is to be followed when installing the Module Creator:

1. We'll get started by going to the extension page on **Magento Connect** for the Module Creator and grabbing the key for this extension.

2. Next, we'll insert the **extension key** from the Module Creator **Magento Connect** extension page at: http://www.magentocommerce.com/extension/1108/modulecreator.

3. We'll open /downloader/ into the input box (at the top of the page) and copy and paste the **extension key** into the input box at the top of the page.

4. We'll proceed by clicking **Install** to install the module into our Magento installation.

```
downloading Netz98_ModuleCreator-1.0.0.tgz ...
Starting to download Netz98_ModuleCreator-1.0.0.tgz (15,542 bytes)
.......done: 15,542 bytes
install ok: channel://connect.magentocommerce.com/community/Netz98_ModuleCreator-1.0.0
```

A success message (similar to the one shown in the previous screenshot) is displayed.

Creating our first module with the Module Creator

We'll start by loading the `/moduleCreator/` in our Magento installation's URL in the browser. A default first screen is displayed, now that it's installed:

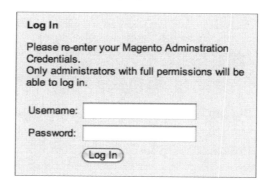

When we log in with the Magento administrative credentials, we'll find ourselves inside the script of the **Module Creator**, and the functionality screen will unveil itself. It will look similar to the following screenshot:

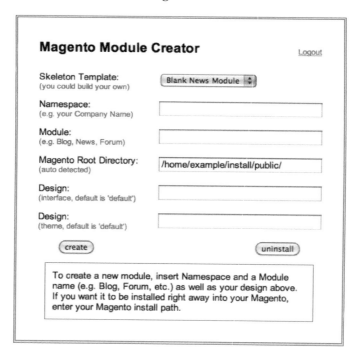

All options are available to us in this initial screen, along with installed skeleton module templates (with scripts). These can be loaded individually if we want to install more later for rapid deployment. We can also develop a **Skeleton Template** on our own, in future.

We'll be using a **Blank News Module**, which is the default available module with the Module Creator extension.

It's important to note that the **Magento Root Directory** field is relevant to the current location of the **Module Creator** directory. If the Module Creator is located at `http://example.com/moduleCreator/` and our Magento installation is located at `http://example.com/`, then we can simply insert `../` as the value for this field and it will work. In most cases, the correct value of this field should insert itself automatically into the input field, so that we do not have to figure out the correct path ourselves.

As we'll be using the default theme for easier display throughout this book, it's advisable to leave the two design fields blank. If we use this Module Creator in our installation with our own theme, these fields will need to be filled in.

For this chapter we'll be using the following:

Field	Value
Namespace	**Book**
Module	**Helloworld**
Magento Root Directory	**../**
Design	
Design	

Next we'll click on **Create**, and the following message gets displayed:

New Module successfully created!

Go to the folder where this file is located. You'll find a new folder called **new**.

Within are all required files for your new module. This folder has the same structure as your Magento installation. Just make sure you replace the `interface` and `theme` folder with your current design path. If you want to add custom DB-fields go to `/new/local/Book/Helloworld/sql/module_setup/mysql4-install-0.1.0.php` and make your changes for line 12 to 14.

Copy `/new/Book_Helloworld.xml to /app/etc/modules/`. If you chose a Magento install directory, all files can be found in their according directory. Implement your module functionality and you're done!

The contents of our new module

The module will create a solid amount of files for us to start with. The Module Creator would have installed the following files:

- `app/etc/modules/Book_Helloworld.xml`
- `app/code/local/Book/Helloworld/Block/Helloworld.php`
- `app/code/local/Book/Helloworld/controllers/IndexController.php`
- `app/code/local/Book/Helloworld/etc/config.xml`
- `app/code/local/Book/Helloworld/Model/Helloworld.php`
- `app/code/local/Book/Helloworld/Model/Mysql4/Helloworld.php`
- `app/code/local/Book/Helloworld/Model/Mysql4/Helloworld/Collection.php`
- `app/code/local/Book/Helloworld/Model/Status.php`
- `app/code/local/Book/Helloworld/sql/helloworld_setup/mysql4-install-0.1.0.php`
- `app/design/frontend/default/default/layout/helloworld.xml`
- `app/design/frontend/default/default/template/helloworld/helloworld.phtml`
- `app/code/local/Book/Helloworld/Block/Adminhtml/Helloworld.php`
- `app/code/local/Book/Helloworld/Block/Adminhtml/Helloworld/Edit.php`
- `app/code/local/Book/Helloworld/Block/Adminhtml/Helloworld/Grid.php`
- `app/code/local/Book/Helloworld/Block/Adminhtml/Helloworld/Edit/Form.php`
- `app/code/local/Book/Helloworld/Block/Adminhtml/Helloworld/Edit/Tabs.php`
- `app/code/local/Book/Helloworld/Block/Adminhtml/Helloworld/Edit/Tab/Form.php`
- `app/code/local/Book/Helloworld/controllers/Adminhtml/HelloworldController.php`
- `app/code/local/Book/Helloworld/Helper/Data.php`
- `app/design/adminhtml/default/default/layout/helloworld.xml`

If we didn't choose a **Magento Root Directory**, we'll need to manually copy the files to their chosen locations, rather than have the installer doing it. The Module Creator will place all the files within a directory called `/new/` within our `/moduleCreator/` folder. If this is the case, then we'll need to copy the files into their duplicate root folders. For example `/moduleCreator/new/app/etc/modules/` would go into `/app/etc/modules/` and we would need to match this structure throughout.

Hello World

Now that we have our module's core files ready, we want to get a simple Hello World message displayed. We'll start by opening: `app/design/frontend/default/default/template/helloworld/helloworld.phtml`.

At the top of the file, we'll find the following:

```
<h4><?php echo $this->__('Module List') ?></h4>
```

We'll change that to `Hello World`:

```
<h4><?php echo $this->__('Hello World') ?></h4>
```

We'll save `helloworld.phtml` and then load `/helloworld` on our Magento installation's installation URL; the following screenshot is displayed:

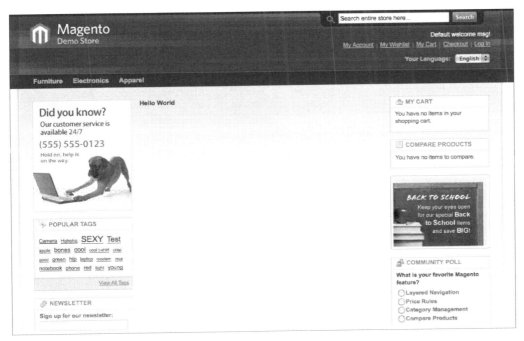

Now we have our **Hello World** using the Module Creator!

Expanding our module further into a database-driven, administrated brands module

We'll now take the development of our module further and create a database-driven list of brands for a section of the site. This part of the chapter will teach us how convert the pieces that we built at the start, into a fully functional module within Magento.

Our module will do the following:

- List a series of brands
- Turn those brands into links, which clicked, show the brand's name and an outline of the location and history of that brand
- Store this data in a database table within the Magento database
- Make it content manageable in the administration of Magento, including adding, editing, and deleting items

Recreating the base

For the sake of making it easier to progress through this chapter, we'll recreate what we did at the start. This will help when we do not want to read everything that we've previously gone through so far. Explanations of these code blocks are at the start of the chapter.

After this, we will add to the base that we've already created earlier in the chapter and introduce a database setup and backend administration into the module.

The directory structure

The directory structure for the module's core files is as follows:

- `/app/code/local/Book/Brands/`
  - `Block/`
  - `controllers/`
  - `etc/`
  - `Model/`
  - `Mysql4/`
  - `Brands/`
  - `sql/`
  - `brands_setup/`

For the module's design template files, we have:

- `/app/design/frontend/default/default/`
    - ◦ `template/`
    - ◦ `brands/`

Enabling the module in the backend

The file `/app/etc/modules/Book_Brands.xml` will be created for our module and it will contain the following:

```xml
<?xml version="1.0"?>
<config>
  <modules>
    <Book_Brands>
      <active>true</active>
      <codePool>local</codePool>
    </Book_Brands>
  </modules>
</config>
```

Our controller

We'll create the file `/app/code/local/Book/Brands/controllers/IndexController.php` and fill it with the following code:

```php
<?php
class Book_Brands_IndexController extends Mage_Core_Controller_Front_
Action
{
  public function indexAction()
  {
    $this->loadLayout();
    $this->renderLayout();
  }
}
```

Configuring the module

We'll create the file /app/code/local/Book/Brands/etc/config.xml and fill it with the following code:

```xml
<?xml version="1.0"?>
<config>
    <modules>
        <Book_Brands>
            <version>0.1.0</version>
        </Book_Brands>
    </modules>
    <frontend>
      <routers>
        <brands>
          <use>standard</use>
            <args>
            <module>Book_Brands</module>
            <frontName>brands</frontName>
            </args>
        </brands>
      </routers>
      <layout>
        <updates>
          <brands>
            <file>brands.xml</file>
          </brands>
        </updates>
      </layout>
    </frontend>
    <global>
      <blocks>
        <brands>
          <class>Book_Brands_Block</class>
        </brands>
      </blocks>
      <helpers>
        <brands>
          <class>Book_Brands_Helper</class>
        </brands>
      </helpers>
    </global>
</config>
```

The Helper model

We'll create the file `/app/code/local/Book/Brands/Helper/Data.php` and place the following code within it:

```php
<?php

class Book_Brands_Helper_Data extends Mage_Core_Helper_Abstract
{
}
```

The module's default model

For the default model, we'll create the file `/app/code/local/Book/Brands/Model/Brands.php` and place the following code within it:

```php
<?php

class Book_Brands_Model_Brands extends Mage_Core_Model_Abstract
{
  public function _construct()
  {
    parent::_construct();
    $this->_init('brands/brands');
  }
}
```

The module's frontend display base

Here we'll put together the template blocks that form the display of this module.

Display block class

We'll create `/app/code/local/Book/Brands/Block/Brands.php` file and place within it the following code:

```php
<?php
class Book_Brands_Block_Brands extends Mage_Core_Block_Template
{
  public function _prepareLayout()
  {
    return parent::_prepareLayout();
  }
  public function getBrands()
  {
```

```
        return 'Brands will go here';
    }
}
```

The layout .xml file

We'll create the file `/app/design/frontend/default/default/layout/brands.xml` and place the following code within it:

```xml
<?xml version="1.0"?>
<layout version="0.1.0">
  <brands_index_index>
    <reference name="content">
      <block type="brands/brands" name="brands" />
    </reference>
  </brands_index_index>
</layout>
```

The design template file

We'll create the file `/app/design/frontend/default/default/template/Brands/brands.phtml` and place the following in it:

```php
<h2><?php echo $this->getBrands(); ?></h2>
```

Extending the base towards introducing a database

Now that we have the base for our brands list, we need to advance it to introduce our database integration.

The configuration .xml file

We'll be editing the existing `config.xml` file to include our database configuration. For shortening the code, existing template tags from the previous `config.xml` file have been shortened with a . . . separator in between them to show that they are unedited.

We'll edit our `config.xml` file to include the following outside of the . . . separators:

```xml
<?xml version="1.0"?>
<config>
  <modules>
    ...
  </modules>
  <frontend>
```

```
    ...
  </frontend>
  <global>
    <models>
      <brands>
        <class>Book_Brands_Model</class>
        <resourceModel>brands_mysql4</resourceModel>
      </brands>
      <brands_mysql4>
        <class>Book_Brands_Model_Mysql4</class>
        <entities>
          <brands>
            <table>brands</table>
          </brands>
        </entities>
      </brands_mysql4>
    </models>
    <resources>
      <brands_setup>
        <setup>
          <module>Book_Brands</module>
        </setup>
        <connection>
          <use>core_setup</use>
        </connection>
      </brands_setup>
      <brands_write>
        <connection>
          <use>core_write</use>
        </connection>
      </brands_write>
      <brands_read>
        <connection>
          <use>core_read</use>
        </connection>
      </brands_read>
    </resources>
    <blocks>
      ...
    </blocks>
    <helpers>
      ...
    </helpers>
  </global>
</config>
```

We'll go into the detail of how `config.xml` and what they do. Our `<models>` tag introduces database specific models that require `mySQL4` in order to operate. This is why we're appending `_mysql4` and `_Mysql4` onto the end of the class names and a `<resourceModel>` tag in the code:

```
<models>
  <brands>
    <class>Book_Brands_Model</class>
    <resourceModel>brands_mysql4</resourceModel>
  </brands>
  <brands_mysql4>
    <class>Book_Brands_Model_Mysql4</class>
    <entities>
      <brands>
        <table>brands</table>
      </brands>
    </entities>
  </brands_mysql4>
</models>
```

The second block of code introduced into `config.xml` covers database resources and what the module will use. This defines that the module has a setup file included that needs to be executed and checked on update. We'll leverage Magento's core setup and write and read database connection settings in order to access the database.

```
<resources>
  <brands_setup>
    <setup>
      <module>Book_Brands</module>
    </setup>
    <connection>
      <use>core_setup</use>
    </connection>
  </brands_setup>
  <brands_write>
    <connection>
      <use>core_write</use>
    </connection>
  </brands_write>
  <brands_read>
    <connection>
      <use>core_read</use>
    </connection>
  </brands_read>
</resources>
```

The mySQL4 data models

We'll create the directory and file /app/code/local/Book/Brands/Model/Mysql4/
Brands.php and place the following code within it:

```php
<?php

class Book_BrandsModel_Mysql4_Brands extends Mage_Core_Model_Mysql4_
Abstract
{
  public function _construct()
  {
    $this->_init('brands/brands', 'brands_id');
  }
}
```

Here we'll expand the core mySQL4 database class within Magento. The second value
in the function $this->_init() should match the Primary Key of our module's
database table.

We'll create the directory and file /app/code/local/Book/Brands/Model/Mysql4/
Brands/Collection.php and place within it the following code:

```php
<?php

class Book_BrandsModel_Mysql4_Brands_Collection extends Mage_Core_
Model_Mysql4_Collection_Abstract
{
  public function _construct()
  {
    $this->_init('brands/brands');
  }
}
```

Just like the previous class, we'll expand Magento's core mySQL classes here, this time
the mySQL Collection class that Magento uses to collect data from the database.

Database setup and installation of the file

In order for our module to store data in the Magento database, we'll need to set up the database in which all the data will be kept, stored, and managed by our backend within Magento.

We'll create the following directory and file `/app/code/local/Book/Brands/sql/` `brands_setup/mysql4-install-0.1.0.php` and place within it the following code:

```php
<?php
$installer = $this;
$installer->startSetup();

$installer->run("

DROP TABLE IF EXISTS {$this->getTable('brands')};
CREATE TABLE {$this->getTable('brands')} (
  `brands_id` int(11) unsigned NOT NULL auto_increment,
  `brand_name` varchar(255) NOT NULL default '',
  `brand_description` text NOT NULL default '',
  `brand_location` varchar(255) NOT NULL default '',
  `status` smallint(6) NOT NULL default '0',
  `created_time` datetime NULL,
  `update_time` datetime NULL,
  PRIMARY KEY (`brands_id`)
) ENGINE=InnoDB DEFAULT CHARSET=utf8;
    ");

$installer->endSetup();
```

Let's run through the code that we've just put together here. We start by assigning the variable `$installer` the current Magento parent class. Then we move onto initializing the installation and calling the child function `startSetup()` to indicate that the setup of the module is being started by the system:

```php
$installer = $this;
$installer->startSetup();
```

We then run the SQL contained within the `run()` function through the system. We'll notice the inclusion of `{$this->getTable('brands')}` in the SQL, which allows us to insert the name of a module table (including any prefix that the Magento installation may have). Any SQL query which is needed for the module later can be included here.

```php
$installer->run("
  ...
  ");
```

The file is then finished off with the `endSetup()` function to complete the install run for the module:

```
$installer->endSetup();
```

Extending the module to include an administration

Now that we have our base and have extended it to include our database integration, we'll take this a step further by including an administration. This is so that we can add, edit, delete, and manage our module's information in the backend of Magento prior to its display.

Adminhtml directories

Let's start by adding a couple of directories into our base in which to place all the files required to add in an administrative backend.

These are contained in `/app/code/local/Book/Brands/`:

```
Block/
    Adminhtml/
        <Module>/
            Edit/
                Tab/
controllers/
    Adminhtml/
```

Administrative display blocks

Magento comes with classes and models for generating the administrative backend for modules. This means that we can input the core information for the screens, and the actual display of the data fields, grids, information, and buttons are output using the currently selected `adminhtml` template in the system.

This automates the processes of paging, exporting data to CSV/XML, filtering data, and searching, thereby saving a lot of work in the development of modules. It also provides a consistent user experience for the users of Magento. The all-round consistency between the modules that users install and use for their Magento installations is a phenomenal benefit provided by this automation.

There are several parts to putting together the administration for this module, which we're going to go over:

- a core model, defining the administration to the system
- an add/edit model, allowing records to be added or edited as needed
- a setup of the module's grid display, for the administrative home page
- a class to declare the edit/add record form
- a class to set the tabs positioned to the left of the edit/add record form when it is being used
- a class to declare fields used in the add/edit record form that appears
- a controller to bring it all together and process accessed URLs for the module in the backend
- the final editing of the config.xml to set up the administrative backend and activate it for our module

While this may seem like a lot of work to get a backend for a module in Magento, it's not as much as would be required for other e-commerce systems (which require us to template every screen and action, as well as creating the models/controllers for our module).

This is also designed to show us everything that can be clubbed together in terms of an administrative backend for our module in Magento. So, we may end up using significantly less for simpler modules that we develop with administrative backends in Magento.

Defining the core administrative backend to the system

To start with, we'll need a model which ensures that the administrative backend is held together and appears in the first place. It also defines our sub-menu item and the labels for the two core buttons on the administrative screen:

- Brand manager (our sub-menu item)
- Add Brand (our **Add New Record** button)

We'll create the file /app/code/local/Book/Brands/Block/Adminhtml/Brands. php and place the following code inside it:

```php
<?php

class Book_BrandsBlock_Adminhtml_Brands extends Mage_Adminhtml_Block_
Widget_Grid_Container
{
```

```
public function __construct()
{
$this->_controller = 'adminhtml_brands';
$this->_blockGroup = 'brands';
$this->_headerText = Mage::helper('brands')->__('Item Manager');
$this->_addButtonLabel = Mage::helper('brands')->__('Add Brand');
parent::__construct();
}
}
```

Let's break up the key lines of this file to make sure everything is understood as we move forward.

We'll start by extending the `Mage_Adminhtml_Block_Widget_Grid_Container` class which is Magento's `Grid` class for displaying grids of information across the backend. We'll also notice that this is used for managing products, orders, customers, newsletter subscribers, and every other type of information that is displayed in a grid in the backend.

```
class Book_Brands_Block_Adminhtml_Brands extends Mage_Adminhtml_Block_
Widget_Grid_Container
```

Defining our controller and `blockGroup` to Magento's `Grid Container` class lets Magento know what controller to look for to process this backend's URLs when accessed. It also declares which folder to look into for the models and the container that we'll be creating to put together in this administrative backend. This is common throughout the code for the administrative setup files.

```
$this->_controller = 'adminhtml_brands';
$this->_blockGroup = 'brands';
```

We'll finish off by defining our `headerText` which appears at the top of the index page for the module's administrative backend and the text used for the `Add Record` button label. This is the common declaration and setting of key labels in the administrative backend and will be used throughout other templates and files in this chapter.

```
$this->_headerText = Mage::helper('brands')->__('Brands Manager');
$this->_addButtonLabel = Mage::helper('brands')->__('Add Brand');
```

Defining the add/edit screens to the system

The following model defines the add/edit screens to the system and sets them up for us.

We'll start by creating the file /app/code/local/Book/Brands/Block/Adminhtml/ Brands/Edit.php and place the following code inside it:

```php
<?php
class Book_Brands_Block_Adminhtml_Brands_Edit extends Mage_Adminhtml_
Block_Widget_Form_Container
{
    public function __construct()
    {
    parent::__construct();

    $this->_objectId = 'id';
    $this->_blockGroup = 'brands';
    $this->_controller = 'adminhtml_brands';

    $this->_updateButton('save', 'label', Mage::helper('brands')->__
('Save Brand'));
    $this->_updateButton('delete', 'label', Mage::helper('brands')->__
('Delete Brand'));
    }

    public function getHeaderText()
    {
    if( Mage::registry('brands_data') && Mage::registry('brands_
data')->getId() ) {
        return Mage::helper('brands')->__("Edit Brand '%s'", $this->html
Escape(Mage::registry('brands_data')->getTitle()));
    } else {
        return Mage::helper('brands')->__('Add Brand');
    }
    }
}
```

Key lines in this code

The line where we defined the objectId to the system, represents the URL key used when the system outputs the /edit/id/5/ URL. When we change the value from id to brand, we'll have the output of /edit/brand/5/.

```php
$this->_objectId = 'id';
```

The `getHeaderText()` function is key in this model, as it provides a way of switching between showing an **Edit Brand** label and an **Add Brand** label depending which screen the user is currently accessing. This is important to understand if we want to change this behavior in any way for our own module.

```
public function getHeaderText()
{
```

If the `_objectId` set earlier appears in the URL, then we'll be on an **Edit Brand** page:

```
    if( Mage::registry('brands_data') && Mage::registry('brands_
data')->getId() ) {
        return Mage::helper('brands')->__("Edit Brand '%s'", $this->html
Escape(Mage::registry('brands_data')->getTitle()));
```

If not, the user will be adding a brand, so the **Add Brand** label is displayed:

```
    } else {
        return Mage::helper('brands')->__('Add Brand');
    }
}
```

The module's grid display declaration

For this class, we'll define the data grid that is displayed when the user clicks on the **Manage Brands** sub-menu item, under our module's administrative backend menu item. Although there's a lot of code to look at, we'll go through it later.

We'll create the file `/app/code/local/Book/Brands/Block/Adminhtml/Brands/Grid.php` and place the following code inside it:

```
<?php
class Book_Brands_Block_Adminhtml_Brands_Grid extends Mage_Adminhtml_
Block_Widget_Grid
{
  public function __construct()
  {
      parent::__construct();
      $this->setId('brandsGrid');
      $this->setDefaultSort('brands_id');
      $this->setDefaultDir('ASC');
      $this->setSaveParametersInSession(true);
  }

  protected function _prepareCollection()
  {
      $collection = Mage::getModel('brands/brands')->getCollection();
      $this->setCollection($collection);
```

```
            return parent::_prepareCollection();
    }

    protected function _prepareColumns()
    {
        $this->addColumn('brands_id', array(
            'header'    => Mage::helper('brands')->__('ID'),
            'align'     =>'right',
            'width'     => '50px',
            'index'     => 'brands_id',
        ));

        $this->addColumn('title', array(
            'header'    => Mage::helper('brands')->__('Title'),
            'align'     =>'left',
            'index'     => 'title',
        ));
        $this->addColumn('status', array(
            'header'    => Mage::helper('brands')->__('Status'),
            'align'     => 'left',
            'width'     => '80px',
            'index'     => 'status',
            'type'      => 'options',
            'options'   => array(
                1 => 'Enabled',
                2 => 'Disabled',
            ),
        ));
          $this->addColumn('action',
              array(
                  'header'    =>  Mage::helper('brands')->__('Action'),
                  'width'     => '100',
                  'type'      => 'action',
                  'getter'    => 'getId',
                  'actions'   => array(
                      array(
                          'caption'   => Mage::helper
                                         ('brands')->__('Edit'),
                          'url'       => array('base'=> '*/*/edit'),
                          'field'     => 'id'
                      )
                  ),
                  'filter'    => false,
                  'sortable'  => false,
                  'index'     => 'stores',
```

```
                   'is_system' => true,
           ));

       return parent::_prepareColumns();
   }
   public function getRowUrl($row)
   {
       return $this->getUrl('*/*/edit', array('id' => $row->getId()));
   }

}
```

There are four core parts to this model's code that we'll learn:

1. The construct.

2. The `prepareCollection()` function, which gathers data from the database ready for display.

3. Preparing the grid's columns.

4. The `getRowUrl()` function.

The __construct()

The `__construct()` function holds the core settings for the module's grid. It starts off by defining the module's grid ID; this is used as an XHTML value applied to the grid to give it a unique identifier. This is useful if we want to do anything with the display by editing the Magento administrative stylesheet.

```
$this->setId('brandsGrid');
```

We'll then move on to defining the default sorting key for the table. In this case, we'll sort by the database table column `brand_name`. We'll set the direction of the order to `DESC`, to make sure that the table records are always in alphabetical order by default.

```
$this->setDefaultSort('brand_name');
$this->setDefaultDir('ASC');
```

The last variable that is set in the `__construct()` function defines whether or not the user's custom filters and parameters applied to this grid should be saved in their session, once they've changed the defaults. This ensures that they can filter by another column, go to another page in the backend, and return with their filter and ordering intact. If set to `false`, the module's grid page will always retain the default settings set in the previous three settings in this function.

```
$this->setSaveParametersInSession(true);
```

Preparing the columns

In the `__prepareColumns()` function, we'll define the columns for display in the grid. We'll define several properties for each field, including the label, which field this label should be displaying, its `width`, `alignment`, field `type`, and (if an option field) its options.

The status field is the best example of this, as it does everything at once:

```
$this->addColumn('status', array(
    'header'      => Mage::helper('brands')->__('Status'),
    'align'       => 'left',
    'width'       => '80px',
    'index'       => 'status',
    'type'   => 'options',
    'options'     => array(
      1 => 'Active',
      0 => 'Inactive',
    ),
));
```

The getRowUrl() function

This function is used to set the URL for any row in the grid, when a user clicks when hovering over a row. The `*/*/edit` defines that the module's namespace and name will appear before the `/edit/` which will begin the URL. It will be then ended with the `$row->getId` variable, to make sure that it forms a good `/edit/id/1` URL to be passed to the system for ensuring that the user is editing the record with the ID 1.

```
public function getRowUrl($row)
    {
    return $this->getUrl('*/*/edit', array('id' => $row->getId()));
    }
```

Preparing the form

This model defines the preparation of our form for loading. It declares the various values of the form (`id`, `action`, and `method`) to the system following the conventions previously outlined in other models.

We'll create the file `/app/code/local/Book/Brands/Block/Adminhtml/Brands/Edit/Form.php` and place the following code inside it:

```
<?php

class Book_Brands_Block_Adminhtml_Brands_Edit_Form extends Mage_
Adminhtml_Block_Widget_Form
```

```
{
    protected function _prepareForm()
    {
    $form = new Varien_Data_Form(array(
        'id' => 'edit_form',
        'action' => $this->getUrl('*/*/save', array('id' => $this-
>getRequest()->getParam('id'))),
        'method' => 'post',
        )
    );

    $form->setUseContainer(true);
    $this->setForm($form);
    return parent::_prepareForm();
    }
}
```

Defining the add/edit form tabs

This module is where the tabs positioned on the left of the form containing different data are set up. In this case we'll only set up one tab, as we don't have enough fields for them to be divided into multiple tabs.

We'll create the file /app/code/local/Book/Brands/Block/Adminhtml/Brands/ Edit/Tabs.php and place the following code inside it:

```
<?php

class Book_Brands_Block_Adminhtml_Brands_Edit_Tabs extends Mage_
Adminhtml_Block_Widget_Tabs
{
  public function __construct()
  {
    parent::__construct();
    $this->setId('brands_tabs');
    $this->setDestElementId('edit_form');
    $this->setTitle(Mage::helper('brands')->__('Brand Information'));
  }

  protected function _beforeToHtml()
  {
    $this->addTab('form_section', array(
      'label'    => Mage::helper('brands')->__('Brand Information'),
      'title'    => Mage::helper('brands')->__('Brand Information'),
      'content'  => $this->getLayout()->createBlock('brands/
adminhtml_brands_edit_tab_form')->toHtml(),
    ));
```

```
        return parent::_beforeToHtml();
    }
}
```

There are two key things going on here in this model. Firstly, in the __construct() function we'll be setting the edit_form as the default form and **Brand Information** as the default title to show when a add/edit form is shown:

```
$this->setId('brands_tabs');
$this->setDestElementId('edit_form');
$this->setTitle(Mage::helper('brands')->__('Brand Information'));
```

Secondly, in the beforeToHtml() function the actual adding of the tab to the form takes place:

```
$this->addTab('form_section', array(
    'label'     => Mage::helper('brands')->__('Brand Information'),
    'title'     => Mage::helper('brands')->__('Brand Information'),
    'content'   => $this->getLayout()->createBlock('brands/
adminhtml_brands_edit_tab_form')->toHtml(),
    ));
```

Here the label and title are both defined as **Brand Information** and we'll make sure to block adminhtml_brands_edit_tab_form, as it's used for the tab's form. This form is declared in the following class.

Configuring and preparing the form for display

Following the tab being declared to show our form block, we'll need to create it. In this model well' creating the form block to be displayed when the form tab we've just declared in the previous file is clicked. We're setting up the fieldsets and fields that are to be used for the form block that appears.

We'll create the file /app/code/local/Book/Brands/Block/Adminhtml/Brands/Edit/Tab/Form.php and place the following code inside it:

```
<?php

class Book_Brands_Block_Adminhtml_Brands_Edit_Tab_Form extends Mage_
Adminhtml_Block_Widget_Form
{
  protected function _prepareForm()
  {
    $form = new Varien_Data_Form();
    $this->setForm($form);
```

```php
$fieldset = $form->addFieldset('brands_form', array('legend'=>Mage
::helper('brands')->__('Brand information')));

$fieldset->addField('brand_name', 'text', array(
  'label'     => Mage::helper('brands')->__('Brand Name'),
  'class'     => 'required-entry',
  'required'  => true,
  'name'       => 'brand_name',
));

$fieldset->addField('status', 'select', array(
  'label'     => Mage::helper('brands')->__('Status'),
  'name'       => 'status',
  'values'    => array(
    array(
      'value'        => 1,
      'label'        => Mage::helper('brands')->__('Active'),
    ),
    array(
      'value'        => 0,
      'label'        => Mage::helper('brands')->__('Inactive'),
    ),
  ),
));

$fieldset->addField('brand_location', 'text', array(
  'label'     => Mage::helper('brands')->__('Location'),
  'class'     => 'required-entry',
  'required'  => true,
  'name'       => 'brand_location',
));

$fieldset->addField('brand_description', 'editor', array(
  'name'         => 'brand_description',
  'label'     => Mage::helper('brands')->__('Description'),
  'title'     => Mage::helper('brands')->__('Description'),
  'style'     => 'width:98%; height:400px;',
  'wysiwyg'   => false,
  'required'  => true,
));

if ( Mage::getSingleton('adminhtml/session')->getBrandsData() )
{
  $form->setValues(Mage::getSingleton('adminhtml/session')-
  >getBrandsData());
  Mage::getSingleton('adminhtml/session')->setBrandsData(null);
} elseif ( Mage::registry('brands_data') ) {
```

```
        $form->setValues(Mage::registry('brands_data')->getData());
    }
    return parent::_prepareForm();
  }
}
```

Three key things happen here. Firstly, we have the `fieldset` that is added at the start:

```
$fieldset = $form->addFieldset('brands_form',
array('legend'=>Mage::helper('brands')->__('Brand Information')));
```

Without this, we can't place the fields anywhere. They need the defined `$fieldset` variable in order to add themselves to the form.

Secondly, the fields are added, in a way remarkably similar to the way they were added to the grid for display previously. We have the same options and a few additional options such as class, which defines the class of the form field and whether or not the field is required upon being input.

Lastly, we have some `callback` functions to the current session in progress to see if they've already tried to fill in this form and failed, therefore needing to place their information back in the form rather than the default:

```
if ( Mage::getSingleton('adminhtml/session')->getBrandsData() )
{
  $form->setValues(Mage::getSingleton('adminhtml/session')-
>getBrandsData());
  Mage::getSingleton('adminhtml/session')->setBrandsData(null);
} elseif ( Mage::registry('brands_data') ) {
  $form->setValues(Mage::registry('brands_data')->getData());
}
```

This function is an extremely useful function to have, in terms of usability and consistency of user experience throughout the Magento administration.

Setting up our brand status array

A standard across Magento modules and other manageable information in the backend is to have statuses assigned to data. For this we'll need to create the file /app/code/local/Book/Brands/Model/Status.php and place the following code inside it:

```
<?php

class Book_Brands_Model_Status extends Varien_Object
{
```

```
const STATUS_ENABLED        = 1;
const STATUS_DISABLED       = 2;
static public function getOptionArray()
{
    return array(
        self::STATUS_ENABLED     => Mage::helper('brands')->__
        ('Enabled'),
        self::STATUS_DISABLED    => Mage::helper('brands')->__
        ('Disabled')
    );
}
}
```

Let's break this down briefly to go over what we've just done.

To start with, we have two constants being declared to define the stored database variables with which Magento will refer to these statuses internally:

```
const STATUS_ENABLED = 1;
const STATUS_DISABLED = 2;
```

After this comes our `getOptionArray()` function which defines our array of status options that we will implement for our module and their variables:

```
static public function getOptionArray()
    {
        return array(
            self::STATUS_ENABLED     => Mage::helper('brands')->__
('Enabled'),
            self::STATUS_DISABLED    => Mage::helper('brands')->__
('Disabled')
        );
    }
```

This passes an array of the following to Magento for our status array:

Value	Label
1	Enabled
2	Disabled

Creating a controller to process access URLs

This controller file will process all the URLs, as they're accessed in the backend. We'll see everything split into functions set up as <name>Action. For example, / module/index/ will be set up as indexAction() and the rest follow the same naming convention.

The code inside this file controls the core actions for these individual URLs and sets the individual pages up for loading.

We'll create the file /app/code/local/Book/Brands/controllers/Adminhtml/ BrandsController.php and place the following code inside it:

```php
<?php

class Book_Brands_Adminhtml_BrandsController extends Mage_Adminhtml_
Controller_action
{
  protected function _initAction()
  {
    $this->loadLayout()
    ->_setActiveMenu('brands/items')
    ->_addBreadcrumb(Mage::helper('adminhtml')->__('Brands Manager'),
Mage::helper('adminhtml')->__('Brands Manager'));
    return $this;
  }

  public function indexAction() {
    $this->_initAction();
    $this->renderLayout();
  }

  public function editAction()
  {
    $brandsId     = $this->getRequest()->getParam('id');
    $brandsModel = Mage::getModel('brands/brands')->load($brandsId);

    if ($brandsModel->getId() || $brandsId == 0) {
      Mage::register('brands_data', $brandsModel);

      $this->loadLayout();
      $this->_setActiveMenu('brands/items');

      $this->_addBreadcrumb(Mage::helper('adminhtml')->__('Brands
Manager'), Mage::helper('adminhtml')->__('Brands Manager'));
      $this->_addBreadcrumb(Mage::helper('adminhtml')->__('Brand
Description'), Mage::helper('adminhtml')->__('Brand Description'));

      $this->getLayout()->getBlock('head')->setCanLoadExtJs(true);
```

```
        $this->_addContent($this->getLayout()->createBlock('brands/
adminhtml_brands_edit'))
            ->_addLeft($this->getLayout()->createBlock('brands/adminhtml_
brands_edit_tabs'));

        $this->renderLayout();
    } else {
        Mage::getSingleton('adminhtml/session')->addError(Mage::helper('
brands')->__('Brand does not exist'));
        $this->_redirect('*/*/');
    }
  }

  public function newAction()
  {
    $this->_forward('edit');
  }

  public function saveAction()
  {
    if ( $this->getRequest()->getPost() ) {
      try {
        $postData = $this->getRequest()->getPost();
        $brandsModel = Mage::getModel('brands/brands');
  if( $this->getRequest()->getParam('id') <= 0 )
              $brandsModel->setCreatedTime(Mage::getSingleton('core/
date')->gmtDate());
 $brandsModel
                ->addData($postData)
                ->setUpdateTime(Mage::getSingleton('core/date')-
>gmtDate())
                ->setId($this->getRequest()->getParam('id'))
                ->save();

        Mage::getSingleton('adminhtml/session')->addSuccess(Mage::help
er('adminhtml')->__('Brand was successfully saved'));
        Mage::getSingleton('adminhtml/session')->setBrandsData(false);

        $this->_redirect('*/*/');
        return;
      } catch (Exception $e) {
        Mage::getSingleton('adminhtml/session')->addError($e-
>getMessage());
        Mage::getSingleton('adminhtml/session')-
>set<Module>Data($this->getRequest()->getPost());
        $this->_redirect('*/*/edit', array('id' => $this-
>getRequest()->getParam('id')));
        return;
```

```
        }
      }
      $this->_redirect('*/*/');
    }

    public function deleteAction()
    {
      if( $this->getRequest()->getParam('id') > 0 ) {
        try {
          $brandsModel = Mage::getModel('brands/brands');

          $brandsModel->setId($this->getRequest()->getParam('id'))
            ->delete();

          Mage::getSingleton('adminhtml/session')->addSuccess(Mage::help
er('adminhtml')->__('Brand was successfully deleted'));
          $this->_redirect('*/*/');
        } catch (Exception $e) {
          Mage::getSingleton('adminhtml/session')->addError($e-
>getMessage());
          $this->_redirect('*/*/edit', array('id' => $this-
>getRequest()->getParam('id')));
        }
      }
      $this->_redirect('*/*/');
    }
}
```

Let's break down the code and go through it so that you understand what we've just done in this file.

We start out by declaring our `BrandsController` class that will hold the `admin` together.

```
<?php

class Book_Brands_Adminhtml_BrandsController extends Mage_Adminhtml_
Controller_action

{
```

Our first function is `_initAction()` which sets the brands/brands manager as active in the menu handler in the backend of Magento as well as setting the breadcrumb trail.

```
    protected function _initAction()
    {
      $this->loadLayout()
      ->_setActiveMenu('brands/items')
```

```
     ->_addBreadcrumb(Mage::helper('adminhtml')->__('Brands Manager'),
  Mage::helper('adminhtml')->__('Brands Manager'));
     return $this;
  }
```

Our `indexAction()` function calls our `_initAction()` function to start and then renders the layout.

```
  public function indexAction() {
     $this->_initAction();
     $this->renderLayout();
  }
```

Next we're putting actions to our edit function.

```
  public function editAction()
  {
```

We grab the get parameter ID and use it to load the brand in our database by that ID.

```
  $brandsId    = $this->getRequest()->getParam('id');
  $brandsModel = Mage::getModel('brands/brands')->load($brandsId);
```

If there's a brand by that ID we're going to set `brands_data` in the Magento global registry.

```
  if ($brandsModel->getId() || $brandsId == 0) {
     Mage::register('brands_data', $brandsModel);
```

Followed by the initializing of the loading for the page layout and setting of the active brand navigation item. We'll then make sure we can load the extra functions in the JavaScript library should we need them.

```
     $this->_initAction();
     $this->_addBreadcrumb(Mage::helper('adminhtml')->__('Brand
  Description'), Mage::helper('adminhtml')->__('Brand Description'));
     $this->getLayout()->getBlock('head')->setCanLoadExtJs(true);
```

The following loads our content for the page which will load the edit form and any tabs that will appear in the left sided navigation of the edit page.

```
     $this->_addContent($this->getLayout()->createBlock('brands/
  adminhtml_brands_edit'))
          ->_addLeft($this->getLayout()->createBlock('brands/adminhtml_
  brands_edit_tabs'));
     $this->renderLayout();
```

If the brand doesn't exist, show an error box with the contents **Brand does not exist** and redirect to the brands index.

```
      } else {
         Mage::getSingleton('adminhtml/session')->addError(Mage::helper('
brands')->__('Brand does not exist'));
         $this->_redirect('*/*/');
      }
   }
```

Our `newAction()` will handle a new brand being inserted. It will call the `editAction()` function and load the form as a new brand instead of one being edited.

```
   public function newAction()
   {
      $this->_forward('edit');
   }
```

The `saveAction()` function will be called once the edit form is posted.

```
   public function saveAction()
   {
```

We'll check if posted information exists, and if it goes grab it and the `brand controller` module to interface with brand information going forward.

```
      if ( $this->getRequest()->getPost() ) {
         try {
            $postData = $this->getRequest()->getPost();
            $brandsModel = Mage::getModel('brands/brands');
```

If we have a brand ID we'll set the record created time to attach to our database entry for the saved brand once inserted.

```
      if( $this->getRequest()->getParam('id') <= 0 )
                  $brandsModel->setCreatedTime(Mage::getSingleton('core/
      date')->gmtDate());
```

Followed by the inserting of the brand into the database.

```
      $brandsModel
                     ->addData($postData)
                     ->setUpdateTime(Mage::getSingleton('core/date')-
      >gmtDate())
                     ->setId($this->getRequest()->getParam('id'))
                     ->save();
```

We then set a success message, remove the saved brand data in the Magento registry and redirect to the brands information index.

```
        Mage::getSingleton('adminhtml/session')->addSuccess(Mage::help
er('adminhtml')->__('Brand was successfully saved'));
        Mage::getSingleton('adminhtml/session')->setBrandsData(false);

        $this->_redirect('*/*/');
        return;
```

If we have an error at any point we'll set an error message and forward back to the brands index.

```
        } catch (Exception $e) {
            Mage::getSingleton('adminhtml/session')->addError($e-
>getMessage());
            Mage::getSingleton('adminhtml/session')->setBrandsData($this-
>getRequest()->getPost());
            $this->_redirect('*/*/edit', array('id' => $this-
>getRequest()->getParam('id')));
            return;
        }
    }
    $this->_redirect('*/*/');
}
```

The final function in the file is that of the function that handles deletion of records, `deleteAction()`.

```
    public function deleteAction()
    {
```

Once again we confirm an `'id'` parameter is set before we continue.

```
        if( $this->getRequest()->getParam('id') > 0 ) {
            try {
```

We then load the brands model and proceed to call the `delete()` function to remove the brand that matches the current set ID.

```
            $brandsModel = Mage::getModel('brands/brands');
            $brandsModel->setId($this->getRequest()->getParam('id'))
                ->delete();
```

We can then set a success message and forward back to the brands index.

```
            Mage::getSingleton('adminhtml/session')->addSuccess(Mage::help
er('adminhtml')->__('Brand was successfully deleted'));
            $this->_redirect('*/*/');
```

If an error occurs we set an error message and go back to the brands index.

```
    } catch (Exception $e) {
        Mage::getSingleton('adminhtml/session')->addError($e-
>getMessage());
        $this->_redirect('*/*/edit', array('id' => $this-
>getRequest()->getParam('id')));
    }
  }
  $this->_redirect('*/*/');
  }
}
```

Next we'll alter our configuration file, so that our XML reflect the code we've just implemented.

Changing the module's config.xml to reflect the administrative backend

Now that we have all our files together for the complete backend administrative display of our module, we'll need to define these blocks and actions in our module's config.xml file. As we used the separator to define tags that remain unchanged to cut down the amount of repeated code.

We'll open /app/code/local/Book/Brands/etc/config.xml and make the following additions:

```
<?xml version="1.0"?>
<config>
    <modules>
        ...
    </modules>
    <frontend>
        ...
    </frontend>
    <admin>
        <routers>
      <brands>
        <use>admin</use>
        <args>
          <module>Book_Brands</module>
          <frontName>brands</frontName>
        </args>
      </brands>
```

```
          </routers>
      </admin>
      <adminhtml>
      <menu>
         <brands module="brands">
            <title>Brands</title>
            <sort_order>71</sort_order>
            <children>
               <items module="brands">
                  <title>Manage Brands</title>
                  <sort_order>0</sort_order>
                  <action>brands/adminhtml_brands</action>
               </items>
            </children>
         </brands>
      </menu>
      <acl>
         <resources>
            <all>
               <title>Allow Everything</title>
            </all>
            <admin>
               <children>
                  <Book_Brands>
                     <title>Brands Module</title>
                     <sort_order>10</sort_order>
                  </Book_Brands>
               </children>
            </admin>
         </resources>
      </acl>
      <layout>
         <updates>
            <brands>
               <file>brands.xml</file>
            </brands>
         </updates>
      </layout>
      </adminhtml>
      <global>
         ...
      </global>
   </config>
```

We'll break down the additions to our `config.xml` file so that they once again make sense as we proceed forward.

The first part defines that we have a controller to handle the URLs in the backend:

```
<admin>
  <routers>
    <brands>
      <use>admin</use>
      <args>
        <module>Book_Brands</module>
        <frontName>brands</frontName>
      </args>
    </brands>
  </routers>
</admin>
```

We then have a starting `<adminhtml>` block tag, which brings in three groups of configuration options to the file, the first of which defines our menu to the administrative backend. It defines the title of the menu item, the sort order (when it should appear in the order of the main menu items), and the sole sub-item in the menu (referred to as children). We'll call it **Manage Brands**:

```
<menu>
  <brands module="brands">
    <title>Brands</title>
    <sort_order>71</sort_order>
    <children>
      <items module="brands">
        <title>Manage Brands</title>
        <sort_order>0</sort_order>
        <action>brands/adminhtml_brands</action>
      </items>
    </children>
  </brands>
</menu>
```

The second of the `<adminhtml>` block tag group defines permissions for our module. It defines which resources should be made available as options to select in the permissions section of setting up a user and what it should allow them access to in the administrative backend. Here we've defined an **Allow Everything** resource group which allows complete access to do anything in our module to the user or user group given the permission:

```
<acl>
  <resources>
    <all>
      <title>Allow Everything</title>
```

```
      </all>
      <admin>
        <children>
          <Book_Brands>
            <title>Brands Module</title>
            <sort_order>10</sort_order>
          </Book_Brands>
        </children>
      </admin>
    </resources>
  </acl>
```

The third and last set of tags in the new `<adminhtml>` block tag of configuration options defines the layout `.xml` file, which provides the display blocks for processing when the URLs are accessed:

```
<layout>
  <updates>
    <brands>
      <file>brands.xml</file>
    </brands>
  </updates>
</layout>
```

This layout `.xml` file is going to be created next in our process.

Giving our administrative backend a layout .xml file

Just like on the front end, we'll need to create a layout `.xml` file for our `adminhtml` files defined for Magento. This pulls everything together and ensures that everything loads properly.

We'll create the file `/app/design/adminhtml/default/default/layout/brands.xml` and place the following inside of it:

```
<?xml version="1.0"?>
<layout version="0.1.0">
  <brands_adminhtml_brands_index>
    <reference name="content">
      <block type="brands/adminhtml_brands" name="brands" />
    </reference>
  </brands_adminhtml_brands_index>
</layout>
```

This will ensure that when we access our module in the backend, it loads as it should through the controller that we created for it earlier and along with all subsequent files.

With the addition of this file, we have ourselves a fully active administrative backend for our module that connects with the database table that we put together earlier.

A look at the administrative backend

Let's take a minute or two to admire what the backend looks like, now that we've put it together and everything is in the system.

In the following screenshot, we'll look at the data display grid:

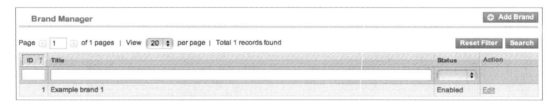

The **Add Brand** form is shown in the following screenshot:

The final stage in this process is making sure all the information from the backend administrative component can output on the frontend of the system, when the URL is accessed. This is done by editing the display block models and template files that we setup earlier in the chapter for both, brands list, and a singular brand view. Here we can use the data that we've put together as needed.

Let's look back at the fields that we set up for our module:

- `brand_id`
- `brand_name`
- `brand_description`
- `brand_location`
- `status`
- `updated_time`
- `created_time`

For our purpose, we'll set up the following:

1. An index loading function, which lists all (active status) brands in the database and when they were last updated.

2. A singular brand loading function, which lists all information that we have on the individual brand being viewed.

The index controller

To start off, we need to ensure that we load the data correctly on the core index and also while viewing the individual brand's page. Here we'll make sure that the data is loaded for it to be used in our template files on the frontend.

We'll open and edit `/app/code/local/Book/Brands/controllers/IndexController.php` file and make sure it looks like the following:

```php
<?php
class Book_Brands_IndexController extends Mage_Core_Controller_Front_
Action
{
  public function indexAction()
  {
    $brands_id = $this->getRequest()->getParam('id');

      if($brands_id != null && $brands_id != '') {
      $brands = Mage::getModel('brands/brands')->load($brands_id)-
>getData();
```

```
        } else {
          $brands = null;
        }

        if($brands == null) {
        $resource = Mage::getSingleton('core/resource');
        $read= $resource->getConnection('core_read');
        $brandsTable = $resource->getTableName('brands');

        $select = $read->select()
          ->from($brandsTable,array('brands_id','brand_
          description','brand_location','status'))
          ->where('status', 1)
          ->order('created_time DESC') ;

        $brands = $read->fetchRow($select);
        }
      Mage::register('brands', $brands);

  $this->loadLayout();
      $this->renderLayout();
    }
  }
```

Let's go through these edits to make sure that everything is clear.

First off, we'll start by assigning $brand the value of $_GET['id']. We'll use this function, as it filters out any cross-site scripting and to eliminate the bad things that can happen to the raw variable, when we use it as we please.

```
    $brands_id = $this->getRequest()->getParam('id');
```

If this value isn't blank (that is, if we're looking at a singular brand's page), then we'll call the load() function from our brands data model. If not, then we set $brands to null for the next bulk of the code that follows.

```
    if($brands_id != null && $brands_id != '') {
    $brands = Mage::getModel('brands/brands')->load($brands_id)-
    >getData();
    } else {
        $brands = null;
    }
```

If $brands == null, then this means that we're not looking at an individual brand page and are looking at the index, which needs to list them all.

```
    if($brands == null){
```

We'll assign the database functions to the variable $resource and make sure that we use the core_read database setup and assigning the brands table name to the variable $brandsTable.

```
$resource = Mage::getSingleton('core/resource');
  $read= $resource->getConnection('core_read');
  $brandsTable = $resource->getTableName('brands');
```

Now we will build the query needed to obtain all brands from the table where status = 1 ordered by the newest created to oldest entries in the table. Status 1 means **Enabled** in this case.

```
$select = $read->select()
  -> from($brandsTable,array('brands_id','brand_description','brand_
  location','status'))
  ->where('status',1)
  ->order('created_time DESC') ;

  $brands = $read->fetchRow($select);
}
```

To finish off, $brands, which is now set to either a group of all the brands or a singular brand, is now registered as a variable which can be accessed across the module further on:

```
Mage::register('brands', $brands);
```

Displaying the brands data

To display the data that we've set by editing our index controller, we'll open and make edits to the module's template file located at the address /app/design/frontend/default/default/templates/brands/brands.phtml. Here's the file after the edits are made:

```
<?php
$brands = $this->getBrands();
if ( count($brands) > 0 )
{
  foreach ( $brands as $brand ) :
    echo '<h3><a href="'.$this->getUrl('brands?id='.$brand['brand_
    id']).'">Name: '.$brand['title'].'</a></h3>';
    echo '<p><strong>Location: '.$brand['location'].'</strong></p>';
    echo '<p>Desciption: '.$brand['brand_description'].'</p><hr />';
  endforeach;
}
else
```

```
{
    print 'We don\'t have any brands here right now. Please try again
    later.';
}
```

We'll go through this code step by step.

We start off by assigning the brands (if we're on the index) or brand (if we use `?id=<brand_id>` on the end of the URL) to the variable `$brands`.

```
$brands = $this->getBrands();
```

We then need to make sure that this is an array. If it isn't, then our data model tells us that the result is not found.

```
if (count($brands)>0)
{
```

If we have a result inside our array (or multiple results), then we go through them in a `foreach` loop and `echo` out simple formatting to display them on the site:

```
foreach ( $brands as $brand ) :
    echo '<h3><a href="'.$this->getUrl('brands?id='.$brand['brand_
    id']).'">Name: '.$brand['title'].'</a></h3>';
    echo '<p><strong>Location: '.$brand['location'].'</strong></p>';
    echo '<p>Desciption: '.$brand['brand_description'].'</p><hr />';
endforeach;
```

However, if we don't have a result inside the array, we'll display a simple message to the person visiting the page that we don't have any brands just yet and that they need to come back a little bit later.

```
}
else
{
    print 'We don\'t have any brands here right now. Please try again
    later.';
}
```

There we go, we have our module's data displaying on the frontend! If we follow all the steps in this chapter, then our brand data display will look as shown in the following screenshot:

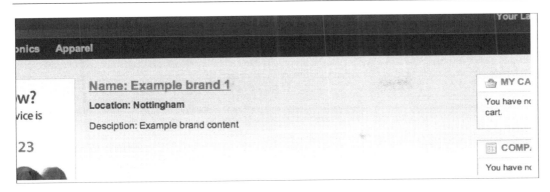

Summary

In this chapter, we've covered the basics of creating an advanced module for Magento. With this knowledge, we will be able to progress onto building more advanced modules in Magento.

We've covered multiple topics on building modules including:

- Setting up the module
- Getting our first **Hello World** output on its own dedicated URL
- Creating a sample module quickly through the Module Creator script
- Altering and editing this sample module to create our very own Brands Management module

After reading this chapter, we should try and enhance it by:

- Adding more fields and information to the brands output
- Splitting brands into pages — for example, 1, 2, 3, 4, and so on
- Giving brands their own singular templates and custom URLs
- Building a form to accept submissions on the brands which people would like to see added onto the site or to take requests
- Allowing users to review brands
- Providing the brands more information than on the listing, for each individual brand page to display

Other small modules we could develop, to use the knowledge gained in this chapter and put it to practical use by analyzing, include:

- A Google maps inclusion module—to include a simple Google map
- A Twitter/Flickr/del.icio.us feed inclusion script
- A basic blog/news system

8
Integration of Third-Party CMS

Sometimes, the built-in content management functionality of Magento isn't enough for our site, or we need a blog or news section in addition to Magento's e-commerce. In some cases, it's the other the way around, and we would like to add Magento's e-commerce functionality to our chosen content management system.

In this chapter we'll go over a few of the content management system integration options available, while focusing on WordPress. We will learn the following:

- Installing the WordPress extension
- Configuring the WordPress extension
- Configuring Magento's display of the WordPress extension
- Changing the look and display of your templates for the WordPress integration
- Which other third party CMS integration packages and extensions for ExpressionEngine, Drupal, Typo3, and Joomla! are available

Notable things about CMS Integration

We must ensure that we back up both our Magento installation and our CMS installation before editing them. Sometimes, the core files are to be edited, and so we'll need to keep a backup of the original version of the files before editing them. Keeping a copy of the database is also advisable.

It's also advisable to back up the files with changes intact after finishing the integration, in case an upgrade of either system knocks the integration out of sync.

The WYSIWYG editor implementation

If we simply want to implement a WYSIWYG editor into our Magento install, there are two available modules that can be installed to integrate this functionality available at the following URLs:

`http://www.magentocommerce.com/extension/586/fontis-wysiwyg-editor.`

`http://www.magentocommerce.com/extension/1426/bouncingorange-tinymce-wysiwyg.`

Integrating Wordpress

In this section, we'll learn about integrating Wordpress with Magento.

 WordPress is an entirely open source, free system available for download by anyone who can navigate to `http://wordpress.org/download/`. Initially built to be a small content management system based around improving typography, WordPress has grown to power hundreds and thousands of blogs worldwide and is the biggest self-hosted blogging tool available on the web today.

Here, we'll install a popular available module by the name of Lazzymonks, a WordPress integration from Magento Connect for integrating WordPress into Magento. It enables the viewing of blog posts and pages within the Magento layout, as well as a sidebar block being included in the module for archives, categories, and RSS feed links to be shown to the users.

Installation

To install the WordPress integration module, we need to make sure that both Magento and WordPress are installed in the same database; otherwise, the module will not work.

Before we start, it must be ensured that our `preferred state` setting is set to `beta`, as this module is currently marked as, in beta development. This can be found under the **settings** tab whilst within the downloader.

We must also ensure that our WordPress installation is installed in a folder named `/wordpress/` in our root Magento installation folder. This is also vital as the extension does not look for any other folder and is currently not configurable to look for folders not named `/wordpress/`.

The module that we'll be installing is located at: `http://www.magentocommerce. com/extension/296/lazzymonks-wordpress-integration`.

Once we find and load the page for the Lazzymonks Wordpress Integration plugin we click on the **Get extension key** button (shown in the previous screenshot) to unveil the extension key for the module. We have to make sure to copy the extension key from the input area for the next step.

Next, we load up our **Magento Connect** downloader located at `/downloader/` from our root installation address or **System->Downloader** in the Magento administration menu. Once we have logged into the downloader, we paste the extension key into the text input located under **Install New Extensions**, as shown in the following screenshot:

The install should be relatively quick:

```
downloading Mage_Blog-0.6.0.tgz ...
Starting to download Mage_Blog-0.6.0.tgz (33,269 bytes)
. . . . . . ...done: 33,269 bytes
install ok: channel://connect.magentocommerce.com/community/Mage_Blog-0.6.0
```

We open `index.php` from our Magento installation folder and find the line:

```
require_once $mageFilename;
```

Next, we place the following code after the above code:

```
define('WP_USE_THEMES', true);
require('./wordpress/wp-blog-header.php');
```

We must make sure that the second line here points to our WordPress installation, otherwise this will break.

After that, we open `/wordpress/wp-settings.php`. We will need to find and remove the `&` symbol from the code. This is to make the code compatible with Magento. The line numbers are placed for a quick reference, roughly related to the latest version of WordPress:

Line 520:

```
$wp_the_query =& new WP_Query();
```

Line 535:

```
$wp_rewrite =& new WP_Rewrite();
```

Line 524:

```
$wp =& new WP();
```

Line 578:

```
$wp_locale =& new WP_Locale();
```

Next, we find the following and comment it out (around `Line 583`):

```
// Escape with wpdb.
$_GET    = add_magic_quotes($_GET   );
$_POST   = add_magic_quotes($_POST  );
$_COOKIE = add_magic_quotes($_COOKIE);
$_SERVER = add_magic_quotes($_SERVER);
```

This results in the following:

```
// Escape with wpdb.
//$_GET    = add_magic_quotes($_GET   );
//$_POST   = add_magic_quotes($_POST  );
//$_COOKIE = add_magic_quotes($_COOKIE);
//$_SERVER = add_magic_quotes($_SERVER);
```

We'll keep them in (rather than removing them), so that it is easier to reverse the changes later if we need to (if we're uninstalling).

Now, we open `wordpress/wp-includes/l10n.php` and find the following (in WordPress 2.7.1, on Line 112):

```
function __($text, $domain = 'default') {
return translate($text, $domain);
}
```

Next, we replace this block of code with the following to allow Magento's translate function to operate, where necessary:

```
if (!function_exists('__')) {
function __($text, $domain = 'default') {
return translate($text, $domain);
}
}
```

That's all for the code edits needed for installation. After we have done this, we will take the `magento` folder from within `/wordpress_module_files/Wordpress-theme/` and place it within our `/wordpress/wp-content/themes/` Wordpress themes folder. This will give WordPress a theme called `Magento`, which allows us to interface with the Magento installation.

Next, we log into our WordPress administration and go to **Appearance->Themes**, where we'll see the Magento theme that is now available:

We click the title to pop up the theme preview and activate it. If we navigate to /wordpress/ directly, we will receive a blank page.

We go to **Settings->General** and change our WordPress URL to our Magento installation URL /blog/. For example, this means that if our Magento installation is at http://localhost/magento/, then our WordPress URL would be http://localhost/magento/blog.

We must make sure to save and then head over to **Settings->Permalinks**. It must be ensured that the **Permalinks** are set to **Default** and turned off entirely; otherwise, this will affect our Magento/WordPress integration. Hopefully better Permalinks will be implemented in a future version of this module.

When we navigate to our newly set WordPress URL, we will see our newly integrated WordPress blog within our store, as shown below:

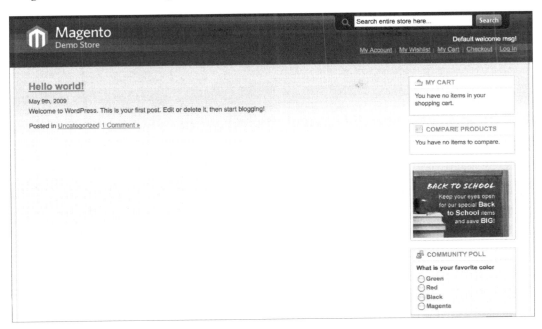

We will also see the blog sidebar block included by default on the right-hand side of our layout:

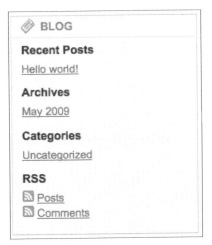

Configuration

Once the install process has finished, we head to our Magento administration system and to **System->Configuration.** We will now see a **Blog** sub-menu that controls our WordPress integration settings for this plugin.

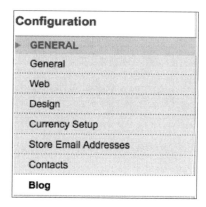

Under this new menu item, we will find all our configuration options for integration that the extension allows within Magento:

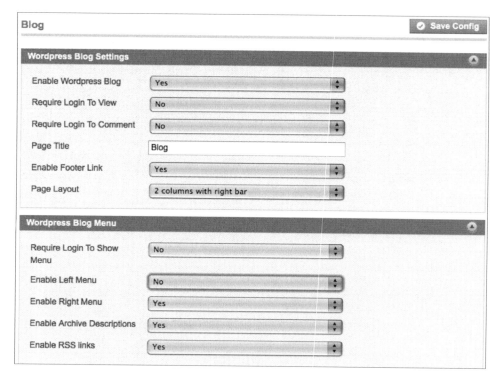

Let's browse through the configuration values so that we could understand what each configuration value does.

WordPress Blog Settings

Configuration value	What it does
Enable WordPress Blog	Enables or disables /blog/ from working
Require Login To View	Requires log in to the Magento user system to view the blog, allows for private member news
Require Login To Comment	Requires log in to the Magento user system to comment on the blog
Page Title	Changes the page title when a user is accessing the blog URL on our Magento installation
Enable Footer Link	Puts the blog automatically into the footer links menu to be dynamically output if we call the function
Page Layout	Decides which Magento page template to use when showing the blog

WordPress Blog Menu

The following table illustrates the configuration values of a blog menu and what they do:

Configuration value	What it does
Require Login To Show Menu	Decides whether or not to show the sidebar to logged out members of our Magento installation.
Enable Left Menu	Determines whether or not the blog sidebar block shows in the left menu (when available)
Enable Right Menu	Determines whether or not the blog sidebar block shows in the right menu (when available)
Enable Archive Descriptions	If enabled, the user will see a statement similar to the following in the blog sidebar block, when browsing a blog archive on the site: **You are currently browsing the blog archives for May, 2009**
Enable RSS links	Determines whether or not to show the links to your blog's RSS feeds in the blog sidebar block. If disabled, they disappear

It's advisable to configure these options (the way we need them now, rather than later) to make sure that everything is set up before we start tweaking the display. Doing so will display the following message:**stop you have to come back later on**.

If we're going to use widgets in our sidebar, rather than editing the sidebar directly, it's recommend to turn off `Enable RSS links` to ensure that we don't have anything pre-appended to the sidebar widget output.

Changing the display of integration

The extension contains base templates which can we change to alter the display of the integration. Templates for the extension can be found in `/app/design/frontend/default/default/template/blog/`.

There are two templates in this directory for alteration:

- `blog.phtml` — For alteration of the blog page template
- `menu.phtml` — For alteration of the sidebar display

Page/post layout

The `blog.phtml` template doesn't consist of much display, only that of an `if/elseif/else` statement to decide the template to be included. It does, however contain the output for the message: **You must be logged in to view the blog** if the option is enabled.

The actual templating of the blog post look and feel is done within the WordPress theme and the `magento.php` template within the theme directory named `magento` that we copied over earlier. Everything is templated the way a normal WordPress theme would be, besides the fact that we don't call `get_header()`, `get_sidebar()`, or `get_footer()` in our templates.

The default `magento.php` template also uses `<?php wp_reset_query();?>`, which must stay at the top of the file no matter what edits we put in place. This function ensures compatibility with Magento and that no errors occur.

Sidebar

The `menu.phtml` template consists of our sidebar block for display in our chosen Magento sidebar, if its turned on. It contains the archive description messages, a widgetized sidebar, and a non-widgetized sidebar.

This means that it will have a default display if we're not using widgets. However, if we use widgets, then it will set a default set of content to display below the widgets that we select.

Let's take this sidebar widget set up as an example; we've put the following widgets into our sidebar under **Appearance->Widgets** under the WordPress administration system:

- Pages
- Links: Blogroll
- Meta
- Search
- Recent Posts

The end result on both the WordPress configuration and the Magento display is shown in the following screenshots:

Here, we notice that the RSS feeds are automatically placed at the bottom as the **Enable RSS link**s option is set to `Enabled` within Magento. Otherwise, we have a perfect display and control for our blog sidebar widget throughout the site. This widgetized sidebar will also stay active throughout the site, not just on `/blog/`.

Other content management systems

There are numerous other content management systems (not covered directly in this book) that can integrate very well with Magento. All these are publically available modules, either for sale or free download, to integrate their systems with Magento. Most of these are third party and their quality has been ensured, prior to their inclusion in this section of the chapter.

Typo3

Typo3 was founded in 2004 and is defined as a professional Web Content Management Framework. It is an open source system and has an estimated install base of 290,000 websites.

TypoGento `http://www.typogento.com` allows for Magento integration into Typo3. It uses both an extension for Typo3 and an extension for Magento to make it work. However, it permits us to install Magento as a component of Typo3 and to display our store seamlessly within Typo3. It uses the Typo3 user system and allows for seamless template customization.

 There is an excellent guide available on how to install TypoGento available at `http://www.typogento.com/need-a-docu/how-to-install-typogento.html`.

Drupal

Drupal is an open source content management system that allows an individual or community to easily publish, manage, and organize a wide variety of content on a website. Tens of thousands of people and organizations are using Drupal to power scores of different websites.

Magento integration with Drupal has been put forward for the Google Summer of Code as an idea: `http://drupal.org/node/236456`. It is yet to be seen how significant the idea will be, but it seems like it is gaining some traction in the Drupal community.

ExpressionEngine

ExpressionEngine is a flexible and a feature-rich content management system that empowers thousands of individuals, organizations, and companies around the world to easily manage their websites.

eeCommerce (`http://eecommerce.com`) implements its own mammoth web services framework to vastly expand the Magento web services API for enabling it to integrate Magento into ExpressionEngine entirely. It currently lists its feature set as a complete solution to integration with ExpressionEngine and Magento.

Joomla!

Joomla! is an award-winning and one of the most popular online CMS today. Joomla! is also open source and offers a mass variety of extensions, with the current catalog standing at 4400 extensions.

Magento bridge (`http://opensource.jira.nl/projects/magento-bridge`) adds a bridge between Joomla! 1.5 and the Magento e-commerce platform. It not only allows for displaying Magento content within the Joomla! component area, but also ships with Joomla! modules and Joomla! plugins. It's available for purchase at €195.

The bridge uses two types of extensions: on the Joomla!-side a backend component helps us to configure the bridge, while a frontend component shows the Magento content inside the Joomla! component area. Joomla! modules are used to show the Magento shopping cart somewhere within our Joomla! template. Also, plugins are available to allow for further integration (search the catalog, user synchronization, and so on).

On the other side, there is a Magento module which is called through web services. This not only allows for flexible development, but also to have Joomla! and Magento installed on separate servers.

Summary

That's the end of our integration of third party content management systems chapter. In this chapter, we have gone through the following:

- How to install the WordPress extension
- How to configure the WordPress extension
- Configuring Magento's display of the WordPress extension
- Changing the look and display of your templates for the WordPress integration
- Which other third party CMS integration packages and extensions for Expression Engine, Drupal, Typo3 and Joomla! are available

Now, you can practice the integration of Magento for your chosen content management systems. Try it out with WordPress as a starter, and maybe give one of the other packages (highlighted towards the end of this chapter) a go and see how they work out for you!

9
Magento's Core API

In this chapter, we'll be covering one of the most documented features of Magento by Varien. Bundled with any default installation of Magento comes a web services API that allows interaction of third party applications and scripts, with several sets of core data. We can use either SOAP or XML RPC protocols to execute Core API calls for interaction with those available in the system.

In this chapter, we will go through the following:

- What the Core API actually does
- What it can be used for
- What APIs we have available to us
- Setting up API access for our scripts
- What methods of using the API we have available to us
- The methods and functions the Core API has available
- Common errors in the API
- A sample implementation of the customer API for creating, updating, deleting, and retrieving customer data from within Magento

What is the Core API?

The Core API is Magento's bundled API (Application Programming Interface) that comes with a default installation. It enables us to build applications that interface with the Customer, Product, and Order data in any Magento installation.

Which Core APIs are included?

Eighteen APIs currently exist in the system:

- Customer API
- Customer's Groups API
- Customer Address API
- Country API
- Region API
- Category API
- Category Attributes API
- Product API
- Product Attributes API
- Product Attribute sets API
- Product Types API
- Product Images API
- Product Tier Price API
- Product links API
- Order API
- Shipment API
- Invoice API
- Inventory API

What do the Core APIs do?

Each API allows us to retrieve, insert, update, or delete data belonging to the appropriate data group with direct code access. This allows us to interface with data by integrating with our thirdparty script or content management system.

Covering everything from customer data to invoicing and shipping to product data, each API has its own purpose. The APIs are gathered into groups that each have their purpose:

- Customer—For import/export of customer details and addresses to/from Magento
  - Customer API
  - Customer's Groups API
  - Customer Address API

- Directory—Retrieving country/regions from within Magento
    ○ Country API
    ○ Region API

- Catalog—For import/export of categories and products to/from Magento
    ○ Category API
    ○ Category Attributes API
    ○ Product API
    ○ Product Attributes API
    ○ Product Attribute sets API
    ○ Product Types API
    ○ Product Images API
    ○ Product Tier Price API
    ○ Product Links API

- Sales—Import/export of orders to/from Magento
    ○ Order API
    ○ Shipment API
    ○ Invoice API
    ○ Inventory API

Prerequisites to using the Core API

The API can be used out of the box as soon as Magento is installed. The only thing required for using the API is user permission, set up in the system for authentication. An account is set up before any script accesses the given APIs. Later on, our script is able to execute all API calls, using the authorization set up (this will be covered in detail later).

Examples of what can be done with the Core API

There are several interesting implementations of the Core API that could be developed into thirdparty CMSs, such as:

- Automatic stock updates from the system to a thirdparty application
- Creating a customer record, invoice, shipment, and updating stock inventory online when an order is placed off-line
- Building an import script for all products, customers, and order data (but not for orders themselves) from an old database or an e-commerce installation
- Automatically syncing stock inventory into the system, when Excel or CSV files are not available

Giving scripts access to the Core API

In order for our scripts to use the Core API, we need to have an authorization from Magento. This involves setting up an API user and API key to be passed to Magento, in order to be allowed to access the API(s) that we would want to use with the script.

Let's start by setting up a role for our API user. A role is Magento's term for a set of access permissions. For example, `Administrator` and `Customer` are two different roles in the standard Magento user system. Here we define our roles in terms of which resources and methods a user could execute in the system, once authenticated in the Core API.

We start by logging into the Magento administration system and going to **System->Web Services->Roles**, as seen in the following screenshot:

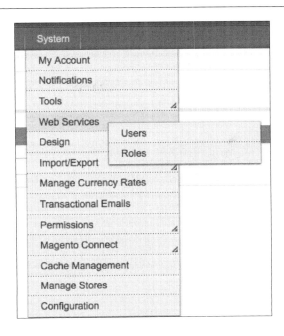

A blank table of roles will be shown initially, as there will be none setup in a default Magento installation. If the roles have been setup beforehand, then we will see roles on the page.

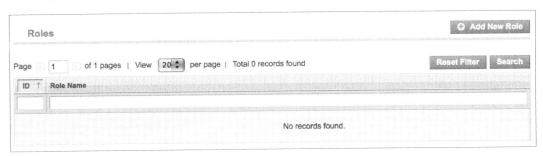

We click on **Add New Role** in the upper-right of the previous screen.

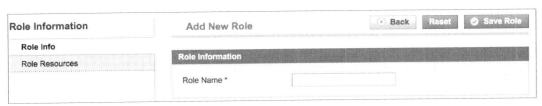

We will immediately see a page that asks for our new **Role Name**. Let's call this one **Complete Access**. Now that we have a name, it's time to assign resources which the role will be allowed to execute when it's connected to our API.

We click **Role Resources** in the left sub-navigation menu to bring up the complete list of resources available which could be assigned to our new role. In this case, we'll select **All** from the **Resource Access** drop-down list (at the top of the page) to give our API role complete access to all resources.

For limiting the role that we're creating (in any way), we can keep the **Resource Access** drop down on **Custom** and tick the boxes applicable to the resources that we would like our role to gain access to, when assigned to a user.

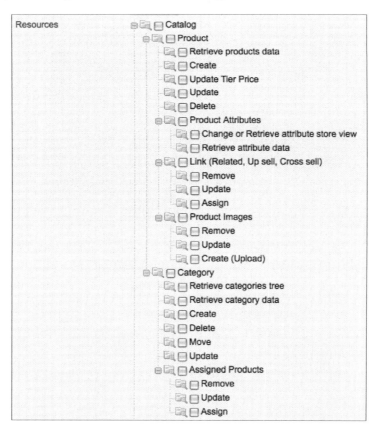

In this example, however, we'll select **All** from the **Resource Access** drop down. We click **Save Role** in the upper-right of the page and head back to our roles index (as we did before). We will see our newly created role on the page.

Next, let's head on over to create the API user to whom this role will apply. We'll go to **System->Web Services->Users**. The **No records found** screen will be displayed unless users have been created previously in the system.

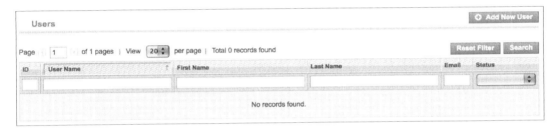

We click **Add New User** in the upper-right side of the screen and progress to the add **New User** screen.

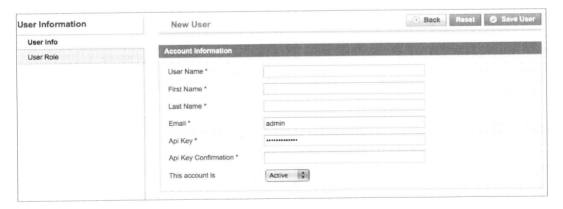

In this screen, we'll be able to set our **User Name** and **Api Key**, required to interface with the API. We can also set our personal information such as **First Name**, **Last Name**, and **Email**. We also have a setting to deactivate the account, (if we ever want to) without deleting it, but for now let's keep it active.

We set values to the following, as this will be used as an example later in the chapter:

Field name	Field value
User Name	Magentobook
First Name	Magento
Last Name	Developer's guide
Email	me@jhuskisson.com
Api Key	Developersguide
Api Key Confirmation	Developersguide
This account is	Active

Once the details are filled in, we click on **User Role** from the sub-menu on the left of the screen and choose the role we created earlier, for our new user.

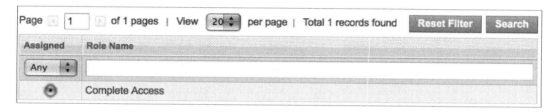

Next, we click **Save User** for the successful creation of our API **User Name** and **API Key** for later use in this chapter. Just for full confirmation, we head back to the **System->Web Services->Users** page to see our new user account appear with all its details.

Now that we're done, we can start experimenting with the API and begin using the methods available to us.

Choice of protocols

Magento provides a couple of choices for the protocol to use with its Core API; these are:

- SOAP
- XML RPC

It's a matter of choice between the two. A few of us would simply decide on preference from previous usage, while some may not be able to use one of the protocols and end up using the alternative. The following information introduces us to both of them, so that we can choose between the two protocols.

SOAP

SOAP is the newer standard of the two and the most popular. It is also faster in comparison and should be our default choice of protocol, if it is available to us.

 More information about the SOAP protocol and its history can be found at: http://en.wikipedia.org/wiki/SOAP or at its official site http://www.w3.org/TR/soap/.

Checking for SOAP installation on the server

Before we're able to use SOAP on our server and therefore use SOAP as the method of interacting with the API, we need to make sure that we have the SOAP PHP extension installed on the server.

To do this, we create a file called `phpinfo.php` and place the following inside it:

```php
<?php
phpinfo();
?>
```

We can save, upload, and access the file directly by inserting the public URL to this file in our browser. Once accessed, we'll see our server's core setup information laid out in front of us, to be devoured! We'll have a look at the following screen titled **soap**.

soap

Soap Client		enabled	
Soap Server		enabled	

Directive	Local Value	Master Value
soap.wsdl_cache	1	1
soap.wsdl_cache_dir	/tmp	/tmp
soap.wsdl_cache_enabled	1	1
soap.wsdl_cache_limit	5	5
soap.wsdl_cache_ttl	86400	86400

Firstly, we'll look for the fact that this SOAP block actually appears. This means that SOAP is installed on the server. If it isn't installed, we'll have to contact our web host or server administrator to get the SOAP PHP extension installed before continuing. If this isn't available to us as an option, we'll have to install XML RPC as the chosen protocol for interacting with the Magento Core API.

Secondly we'll look inside the block at the first setting **Soap Client**. This shows whether or not we're able to execute SOAP clients from our web server. If set to **enabled**, it means that it is installed and we can go ahead with using SOAP as the method of choice. If set to **disabled**, we'll need to contact our web host or web administrator and make sure that they set it to **enabled**.

Putting SOAP to use

If the SOAP PHP extension is installed and enabled on our server, then we'll be able to use the SOAP API provided by the Magento Core API without any external libraries of any kind. Magento's Core API documentation outlines a basic example of usage, shown below:

```
$client = new SoapClient('http:// example.com/api/soap/?wsdl');

// If somestuff requires api authentification,
// we should get session token
$session = $client->login('apiUser', 'apiKey');

$result = $client->call($session, 'somestuff.method');
$result = $client->call($session, 'somestuff.method', 'arg1');
```

```
$result = $client->call($session, 'somestuff.method', array('arg1',
'arg2', 'arg3'));
$result = $client->multiCall($session, array(
    array('somestuff.method'),
    array('somestuff.method', 'arg1'),
    array('somestuff.method', array('arg1', 'arg2'))
));

// If you don't need the session anymore
$client->endSession($session);
```

The key line is the first one, which defines our `SoapClient` for usage of the API:

```
$client = new SoapClient('http://example.com/api/soap/?wsdl');
```

Between the SOAP and XML RPC implementation (in terms of code), this last line is the only line that is different. It is used to initiate the connection to the Magento Core API and attach an instance of the Core API class to the `$client` variable. For example, the function `call()` will now be accessed via `$client->call()`, now that this variable is assigned properly. We must ensure to use the IP address of our computer (rather than `localhost`), if we encounter issues, as some versions of PHP are affected by a problem which stops this call from working properly.

Zend Framework SOAP Client

If we prefer using Zend Framework for everything to retain consistency throughout all of our code in development with Magento, then Zend Framework has a SOAP Client class. We could use it with Magento Core API, available at the following URL:

```
http://framework.zend.com/manual/en/zend.soap.client.html
```

XML RPC

XML RPC is a fantastic fallback, if SOAP is not available on our web host. Although it's slightly slower, it's by all accounts a very solid protocol for accessing the Core API.. By no means is it a different set of code or executions from SOAP.

 More information about XML RPC and its history can be obtained at http://en.wikipedia.org/wiki/XML-RPC or at its official site http://www.xmlrpc.com/.

Getting XML RPC on our server

With XML RPC, there's no need to install anything on our server to get it to work. With our implementation, we'll work with Zend Framework's XML RPC client class to simplify things across the board. What this class does for us is that it provides an exact match of the SOAP interaction of calling methods and brings consistency between the methods of using the API.

 More about Zend Framework XML RPC class can learned at:
`http://framework.zend.com/manual/en/zend.xmlrpc.html`.

Setting up the Zend Framework XML RPC class

Before we can use anything related to XML RPC, we need the Zend Framework XML RPC class. We'll be using this particular class for two reasons:

1. For consistency between code from Magento and custom modules
2. Simply to make sure that we're using the same framework for everything throughout book

We can still use whichever class we choose to with the XML RPC API, as it isn't limited to the class we're using to interact with it.

We start by heading over to `http://framework.zend.com/download/current/` and downloading the minimal package with just the Zend Framework files. We would not want any tests, demos, or Dojo Toolkit clogging up our time when uploading afterwards.

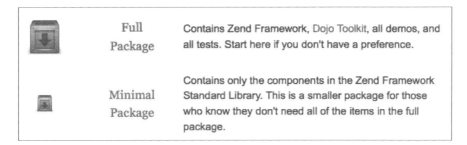

| | Full Package | Contains Zend Framework, Dojo Toolkit, all demos, and all tests. Start here if you don't have a preference. |
| | Minimal Package | Contains only the components in the Zend Framework Standard Library. This is a smaller package for those who know they don't need all of the items in the full package. |

Once we have the minimal package, we place the extracted Zend directory in the same directory as the planned script that will use the Magento Core API. We use the following lines of code for including the class:

```
require_once 'Zend/XmlRpc/Client.php';
```

This will give us everything that we need to start putting the Magento Core API XML RPC protocol to use.

Putting XML RPC to use

Magento's provided XML RPC documentation is as follows:

```
$client = new Zend_XmlRpc_Client('http://example.com/api/xmlrpc/');

// If somestuff requires api authentification,
// we should get session token
$session = $client->call('login', array('apiUser', 'apiKey'));

$client->call('call', array($session, 'somestuff.method',
array('arg1', 'arg2', 'arg3')));
$client->call('call', array($session, 'somestuff.method', 'arg1'));
$client->call('call', array($session, 'somestuff.method'));
$client->call('multiCall', array($session,
    array(
        array('somestuff.method', 'arg1'),
        array('somestuff.method', array('arg1', 'arg2')),
        array('somestuff.method')
    )
));

// If you don't need the session anymore
$client->call('endSession', array($session));
```

The important line of this example is the initial one:

```
$client = new Zend_XmlRpc_Client('http://example.com/api/xmlrpc/');
```

This is the only line that is different from the SOAP protocol example in the code. This is what initializes the XML RPC connection to the Magento Core API and allows us to start executing calls to interact with Magento.

Basic API methods

Magento provides a set of methods, or functions, that we can use once we have our API $client set and ready to use. These methods are the standard for performing calls to the Core API and are the standard for using the Core API with your scripts.

Describing the methods

Here are the Basic API methods as outlined by Magento's Core API guide introduction page:

Method	Description	Return value
startSession()	starts API session and returns sessionId	string
endSession(sessionId)	ends API session	boolean
login(apiUser, apiKey)	starts API session, returns sessionId and authorizes apiUser	string
call(sessionId, resourcePath, array arguments)	calls API resource that is allowed in current session (if no session is specified, you can call only resources that are not protected by ACL)	Mixed
multiCall(sessionId, array calls, array options)	calls API resource's methods that are allowed for current session (if no session is specified, you can call only resources that are not protected by ACL). If break option is specified, multiCall breaks on first error	array
resources(sessionId)	returns list of available API resources and methods allowed for current session.	array
globalFaults(sessionId)	returns list of fault messages and their codes that do not depend on any resource.	array
resourceFaults(sessionId, resourceName)	returns list of the specified resource fault messages, if this resource is allowed in current session.	array

Understanding the methods individually

We'll go through these methods individually, so that we can properly understand them before moving forward.

The following methods are designed to be used separately in each of the code examples given. We must remember to separate them and not combine them one after the other, when trying them out for the first time.

startSession()

This method is used to start a session where API authorization isn't required to access a resource. It's a great option for those building their own APIs for modules, that allow sharing the Magento installation's data with anyone who wants to work on the API.

A sample usage is as follows:

```
// API opening
$session = $client->call('startSession');
// API calls and other actions
// Ending of the session
```

The $session variable is populated with our session ID for use later with other methods and throughout the rest of the script, though in this scenario we won't have many resources to work with. We can try calling the resources method, to see just how many we can access.

endSession(sessionId)

Used to end the API session at the end of our script, to make sure that the API session has been ended properly.

A sample usage is described below:

```
// API opening
// API session start
// API calls and other actions
$client->call('endSession', array($session));
```

This would be placed at the end of our API usage script. The variable $session would be set either via the startSession() method or returned via the login method at the start of our script. This array is then passed to our endSession() method at the end of the script. It's important to end sessions for cleaning up the data that is being stored while the session is in progress.

login(apiUser, apiKey)

This method is used to authenticate your script with Magento using your API user and key.

The following is a sample of its usage:

```
// API opening
$session = $client->call('login', array('Magentobook',
'Developersguide'));
// API calls and other actions
// Ending of the session
```

The `$session` variable is populated with our session ID for use later with other methods and throughout the rest of the script.

call(sessionId, resourcePath, array arguments)

This is used to call API methods one at a time; it is likely to be the most popular method that we will use, while working with the Magento Core API. The following examples demonstrate its usage.

Example one, no arguments needed for a call:

```
$customers = $client->call($session, 'customer.list');
```

Example two, single argument for a call:

```
$client->call($session, 'customer.delete', $CustomerId);
```

Example three, multiple arguments for a call:

```
$calls = array(
    array( 'catalog_product.info', 1 ),
    array( 'catalog_product.info', 2 ),
    array( 'catalog_product.info', 3 ),
);
$results = $client->multiCall( $session, $calls );
```

We notice that the `$session` variable is required for all calls, and that a called function is executed in the format of: `$client->call($session, $resource, $arguments);` no matter which variation of the method is being used.

multiCall(sessionId, array calls, array options)

This is used for batch calls, if ever required. It is similar to the previous call method, but is used for calling several methods at the same time.

It can be used as follows:

```
$client->call('multiCall', array($session,
    array(
        array('somestuff.method', 'arg1'),
        array('somestuff.method', array('arg1', 'arg2')),
        array('somestuff.method')
    )
));
```

This method is best used when mass updating records or if we like to tidy up multiple actions into one statement. For example, when inserting an order with a shipment and invoice all at the same time while importing from another installation.

resources(sessionId)

This method returns a list of the available methods relating to the current session.

The following is an example of its usage:

```
$resources = $client->resources($session);
```

This will return an array of available resources to our current session. Jisse Reitsma of Jira ICT wrote the following code to produce a simple output of all the resources and methods returned by the method, which helps us visualize the output better:

```
<?php if( is_array( $resources ) && !empty( $resources )) { ?>
<?php foreach( $resources as $resource ) { ?>
<h1><?php echo $resource['title']; ?></h1>
Name: <?php echo $resource['name']; ?><br/>
Aliases: <?php echo implode( ',', $resource['aliases'] ); ?>
<table>
    <tr>
        <th>Title</th>
        <th>Path</th>
        <th>Name</th>
    </tr>
    <?php foreach( $resource['methods'] as $method ) { ?>
    <tr>
        <td><?php echo $method['title']; ?></td>
        <td><?php echo $method['path']; ?></td>
```

```
        <td><?php echo $method['name']; ?></td>
        <td><?php echo implode( ',', $method['aliases'] ); ?></td>
    </tr>
    <?php } ?>
</table>
<?php } ?>
<?php } ?>
```

This call is useful when debugging the existing session and can save a lot of heartache when trying to figure out why a resource or method is not executing properly!

globalFaults(sessionId)

This method returns global faults with our API usage. It's useful for seeing which global API faults are occurring, if anything goes wrong. The complete list of these faults can be found later in this chapter.

It is used as follows:

```
$faults = $client->globalFaults($session);
```

This sets $faults to an array of the global faults currently occurring. You can then use a foreach() function to get the faults out of the array for a comfortable display and easy reading.

resourceFaults(sessionId, resourceName)

This returns faults for a specific resource.

It is used as follows:

```
$faults = $client->resourceFaults($session, 'resource.name');
```

This then sets an array of faults for the resource.name resource to the variable $faults, on which we can then use the foreach() function for reading on the front end.

Global API Faults

The following are global Core API fault codes that can be returned, no matter what Core API is being used or which call we execute. These errors apply to each Core API call available. The support guide outlines them as follows:

Fault Code	Fault Message
0	Unknown Error
1	Internal Error. (For details, we can read the log file)
2	Access denied
3	Invalid API path
4	Resource path is not callable
5	Session expired, re-login

These will be directly in PHP error format, if the server allows error reporting when they occur, as shown below:

Fatal error: Uncaught SoapFault exception: [2] Access denied. in /Applications/MAMP/htdocs/api-scripts /api.php:5 Stack trace: #0 [internal function]: SoapClient->__call('login', Array) #1 /Applications /MAMP/htdocs/api-scripts/api.php(5): SoapClient->login('incorrect-usern...', 'incorrect-passw...') #2 {main} thrown in **/Applications/MAMP/htdocs/api-scripts/api.php** on line **5**

In the following table, we can see what these errors are and why they occur:

Fault Code	Reason for fault
0	This error is rare and it normally means something extraordinary has gone wrong.
1	If we read the log, we will come to know exactly what has gone wrong to cause this error.
2	When we called login, we passed an incorrect API user and key combination or the API key and user that we passed to the method does not have rights to call the API method that we're trying to execute.
3	The API path that we had called at the start of our script is invalid and does not exist.
4	The resource that we're trying to call in our function is not callable by our API key and user, or simply does not exist.
5	Our API session has expired and we need to log in again.

In the following table, we have the two fault tables together for a quick overview:

Fault Code	Fault Message	Reason for fault
0	Unknown Error	This error is rare and it normally means something extraordinary has gone wrong.
1	Internal Error. Please see log for details	If we read the log, we will come to know exactly what has gone wrong to cause this error.
2	Access denied	When we called `login`, we passed an incorrect API user and key combination or the API key and user that we passed to the method does not have rights to call the API method that we're trying to execute.
3	Invalid API path	The API path that we had called at the start of our script is invalid and does not exist.
4	Resource path is not callable	The resource that we're trying to call in our function is not callable by our API key and user, or simply does not exist.
5	Session expired, re-login	Our API session has expired and we need to log in again.

Basic API scripting: Customer API

We start with some basic API scripting to ease us into the operations of the Magento Core API, starting with the Customers API.

Getting started

Most of us would be using SOAP, but this is easily interchangeable with XML RPC (as mentioned earlier in the chapter). We start by setting up our connection to the API, creating a file called `api.php`, and placing in it the following:

```php
<?php
$client = new SoapClient('http://m.jhuskisson.com/api/soap/?wsdl');
$session = $client->login('Magentobook', 'Developersguide');
$client->endSession($session);
?>
```

Once we've loaded it into our browser, we'll see a blank screen which means that everything is working nicely.

Creating a customer

We start by creating a customer in our database; we have data in our default Magento installation at the moment. Hence, we'll need to insert customers before we have any data to retrieve or update. Between our `login()` and `endSession()` functions we'll enter:

```
$customerInfo = array(
    'firstname'  => 'First',
    'lastname'   => 'Last',
    'email'      => 'test@example.com',
    'password_hash'   => md5('password'),
    'store_id'   => 0,
    'website_id' => 0
);

$newCustomerId = $client->call($session, 'customer.create',
array($customerInfo));
```

We reload our file in the browser and it should take slightly longer to load, but will still return a blank screen. However, if we take a look at the **Manage Customers** screen under **Customers->Manage Customers** in the Magento administration, we'll see that the new customer has been created successfully.

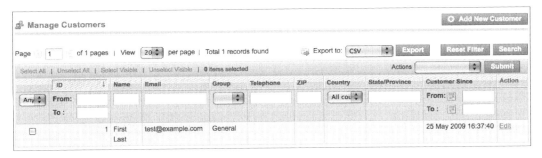

We'll also be able to log in as this newly created customer with the e-mail and password inserted straightaway.

Retrieving an individual customer's details

Now that the customer is in the database, we can retrieve the fictional customer's details using the `customer.info` call and the ID of that customer. For example:

```
$customerId = 1;
$customerInfo = $client->call($session, 'customer.info', $customerId);
print var_dump($customerInfo);
```

Once we save our file and reload the page, we'll see an array output with all the variables applicable to this customer's core data.

```
array(12) {
    ["customer_id"]=> string(1) "1"
    ["created_at"]=> string(19) "2009-05-25 16:37:40"
    ["updated_at"]=> string(19) "2009-05-25 16:37:40"
    ["increment_id"]=> string(9) "000000001"
    ["store_id"]=> string(1) "0"
    ["website_id"]=> string(1) "0"
    ["created_in"]=> string(5) "Admin"
    ["email"]=> string(16) "test@example.com"
    ["firstname"]=> string(5) "First"
    ["group_id"]=> string(1) "1"
    ["lastname"]=> string(4) "Last"
    ["password_hash"]=> string(32) "5f4dcc3b5aa765d61d8327deb882cf99"
}
```

Updating the customer's details

We can use this how we like. In our current situation, we can change the name of this customer via the API, assuming that we have updated it elsewhere away from Magento. To do this, we should use the following code:

```
$newCustomerInfo = array(
    'firstname'  => 'Updated',
    'lastname'   => 'Customer'
);

$client->call($session,
        'customer.update',
        array($customerId, $newCustomerInfo)
        );

var_dump($proxy->call($session, 'customer.info', $customerId));
```

This will update our customer and print out his new details for us to confirm that it works. If our script has worked, we'll see the customer record updated in Magento, as well as a new array printed out of the customer's data that shows the new information.

Listing all customers from the database

In some cases, we may need to get several customers out of the database rather than just the one. Maybe we're inserting the information from the customer database of Magento into another database or need to use it in some way. Magento's Customer API provides a simple way of doing this, as follows:

```
$customerList = $client->call($session, 'customer.list');
```

This will return an array of all customers in the database, for us to process through. It will output exactly how `customer.info` outputs, but in separate arrays for each customer returned via the method.

Deleting a customer from the database

Lastly, if we want to delete a customer record from the Magento database there's a method available, (provided we know the customer ID):

```
$client->call($session, 'customer.delete', $customerID);
```

It's as simple as that; the customer with the ID contained in the `$customerID` variable will be deleted from the database.

Complete list of available resources and methods

The following is a complete list of all the available resources, APIs, and methods in the Magento Core API for quick reference.

> For full reference with example code for each of the APIs, we can visit: `http://www.magentocommerce.com/wiki/doc/webservices-api/api` online.

Customer methods

For handling of customer information in Magento's database, the following methods are available:

Customer API	Customer Groups API
Resource name: customer	**Resource name:** customer_group
customer.list — Retrieve customers	customer_group.list — Retrieve customer's groups
customer.create — Create customer	
customer.info — Retrieve customer data	
customer.update — Update customer data	
customer.delete — Delete customer	
Customer Address API	
Resource name: customer_address	
customer_address.list — Retrieve customer addresses	
customer_address.create — Create customer address	
customer_address.info — Retrieve customer address	
customer_address.update — Update customer address	
customer_address.delete — Delete customer address	

Directory methods

For retrieval of region and country information from Magento's database, the following methods can be used:

Country API	Region API
Resource name: country	**Resource name:** region
country.list — List of countries	region.list — List of regions in specified country

Catalog methods

For handling catalog-related information in Magento's database, we have:

Category API
Resource name: `category`
`category.currentStore`—Set/Get current store view
`category.tree`—Retrieve hierarchical tree
`category.level`—Retrieve one level of categories by website/store view/parent category
`category.info`—Retrieve category data
`category.create`—Create new category
`category.update`—Update category
`category.move`—Move category in tree
`category.delete`—Delete category
`category.assignedProducts`—Retrieve list of assigned products
`category.assignProduct`—Assign product to category
`category.updateProduct`—Update assigned product
`category.removeProduct`—Remove product assignment

Category attributes API	Product API
Resource name: `category_attribute`	**Resource name:** `product`
`category_attribute.currentStore`—Set/Get current store view	`product.currentStore`—Set/Get current store view
`category_attribute.list`—Retrieve category attributes	`product.list`—Retrieve products list by filters
`category_attribute.options`—Retrieve attribute options	`product.info`—Retrieve product
	`product.create`—Create new product
	`product.update`—Update product
	`product.setSpecialPrice`—Set special price for product
	`product.getSpecialPrice`—Get special price for product
	`product.delete`—Delete product

Product attributes API	Product attribute sets API
Resource name: `product_attribute`	**Resource name:** `product_attribute_set`
`product_attribute.currentStore`— Set/Get current store view `product_attribute.list`—Retrieve attribute list `product_attribute.options`—Retrieve attribute options	`product_attribute_set.list`— Retrieve product attribute sets
Product types API	**Product Images API**
Resource name: `product_type`	**Resource name:** `product_attribute_media`
`product_type.list`—Retrieve product types	`product_attribute_media.currentStore`—Set/Get current store view `product_attribute_media.list`—Retrieve product image list `product_attribute_media.info`—Retrieve product image `product_attribute_media.types`—Retrieve product image types `product_attribute_media.create`— Upload new product image `product_attribute_media.update`—Update product image `product_attribute_media.remove`—Remove product image

Product Tier Price API	**Product links API**
Resource name: `product_attribute_tier_price`	**Resource name:** `product_link`
`product_attribute_tier_price.info` — Retrieve product tier prices	`product_link.list` — Retrieve linked products
`product_attribute_tier_price.update` — Update product tier prices	`product_link.assign` — Assign product link
	`product_link.update` — Update product link
	`product_link.remove` — Remove product link
	`product_link.types` — Retrieve product link types
	`product_link.attributes` — Retrieve product link type attributes

Sales methods

For invoices, shipments and credit memos in Magento's database, we have:

Order API	**Shipment API**
Resource name: `order`	**Resource name:** `order_shipment`
`order.list` — Retrieve list of orders by filters	`order_shipment.list` — Retrieve list of shipments by filters
`order.info` — Retrieve order information	`order_shipment.info` — Retrieve shipment information
`order.addComment` — Add comment to order	`order_shipment.create` — Create new shipment for order
`order.hold` — Hold order	`order_shipment.addComment` — Add new comment to shipment
`order.unhold` — Unhold order	`order_shipment.addTrack` — Add new tracking number
`order.cancel` — Cancel order	`order_shipment.removeTrack` — Remove tracking number
	`order_shipment.getCarriers` — Retrieve list of allowed carriers for order

Invoice API

Resource name: `order_invoice`

`order_invoice.list` — Retrieve list of invoices by filters

`order_invoice.info` — Retrieve invoice information

`order_invoice.create` — Create new invoice for order

`order_invoice.addComment` — Add new comment to shipment

`order_invoice.capture` — Capture invoice

`order_invoice.void` — Void invoice

`order_invoice.cancel` — Cancel invoice

Inventory methods

For updating of stock and inventory for products in Magento's database, we have:

Inventory API

Resource name: `product_stock`

`product_stock_item.list` — Retrieve stock data by product ids

`product_stock_item.update` — Update product stock data

Summary

In this chapter, we've learned about interacting with the Magento Core API and the mass database of data that Magento holds. It's certainly a great addition to the excellent e-commerce system that is Magento Commerce.

We have gone through the following:

- What the Core API actually does
- What it can be used for
- What APIs are available to us
- Setting up API access for our scripts
- What methods of using the API we have available to us
- The methods and functions the Core API has available
- Common errors in the API
- A sample implementation of the customer API for creating, updating, deleting, and retrieving customer data from within Magento

With this knowledge, we should be able to write scripts using the Magento Core API. We must take up the challenge of integrating with a third-party system, for testing our newly acquired knowledge of Magento Core API.

10
Importing and Exporting Data

In this chapter, we will learn about the built-in method of getting your data in and out of Magento. Magento is delivered with a set of features aimed at making it easy to get certain types of data in and out of the system. With the import/export functionality, we can set up profiles which act as saved records, so that we can regularly import and export the same data. In practice, this means that if we wish to do that process regularly, then we can set up a profile which will ensure that we don't need to run the filters each time. We can then come back to this, which acts as a save point for all the settings set up previously for the data import/export action.

Here we'll be looking at the profiles that are set up with the system by default, and how we can add our own for easy import/export of data.

What kind of data can I export or import?

Magento has the following default Import/Export data profiles that come with the default installation and what data they relate to:

- Customer data (users who have signed up for the system)
- Product stock data (product stock data only)
- Product data (all attributes relating to products)

 It's worth increasing the value of the PHP `max_execution_time` directive, as product databases over 200-300 products will experience issues with script timeouts on certain web hosting.

There are two types of files that can be used for import/export in Magento:

- Excel Spreadsheet
- CSV (Comma Separated Values)

The typical process is as follows:

1. Creating a new profile
2. Naming the profile and choosing direction (import/export)
3. Choosing a data type
4. Configuring the data type (for example with CSV, we choose tabular or comma separated values)
5. Choosing which type of system data we want to interact with (customers or products)
6. Filtering this data to meet our needs
7. Saving our work
8. Running the profile to produce the desired result

Developers can also export their profiles as XML, in order to advance them under the **Advanced Profiles** functionality that comes with Magento. If we'd like to advance a profile further than the profile builder tool allows, then we can export the profile as XML to tweak into an `Advanced Profile` with more advanced actions.

An introduction to the interface

Profiles can be found under the **Import/Export** menu, in **System->Import/ Export-> Profiles**. Initially, we'll see a screen displaying all the profiles that we have set up, as follows:

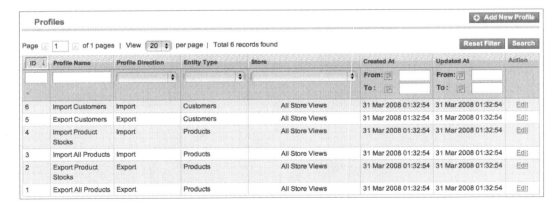

The default profiles that come with Magento (shown in the previous screenshot) cover the **Import/Export** of **Customers**, **Product**, and **Product Stocks**. These will help us get started with the feature and can also act as a template for profiles that will be set up later.

We start with opening **Export Product Stocks,** profile **ID 2**. At the bottom left-hand side of the screen, we see four sections: **Profile Wizard**, **Run Profile**, **Profile Actions XML**, and **Profile History**. These can be seen when exporting data; an additional tab named **Upload File** appears when importing data.

The four sections can be summarized as follows:

- **Profile Wizard** is where we set up the profile through an interface aimed at not having us do any of the XML involved with Advanced Profiles.
- **Upload File** allows us to upload files to be executed through the profile.
- **Run Profile** allows us to run the current profile, as it was last saved.
- **Profile Actions XML** allows us to take the raw XML that makes up this profile and take it into the **Advanced Profiles** section for advancement with options that aren't available via the **Profile Wizard** interface.
- **Profile History** shows us actions previously performed with this profile.

Profile Wizard

We will focus on the **Profile Wizard**, as it is where the core of the **Import/Export** profile feature is based. Let's run through our fields on this tab, which is the default.

Profile Information

Profile Information comprises the following components, shown in the screenshot:

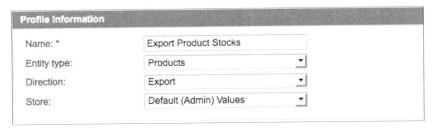

Name

The name that we assign to our profile in order to locate it later on from within the system.

Entity type

This decides which fieldset we interact with for the profile. It takes the options, **Products** and **Customers**. For example, if we select **Products**, then the fieldset for **Products** from the selected store(s) will be loaded for interaction with the actions and methods as selected in the rest of the form.

Direction

This decides the direction of which we're using the data for the profile. For example, whether we'll be taking a file and importing the data using the profile, or we'll be taking the data output from the profile and exporting to a file. It takes the options **Import** and **Export**.

Upon selecting **Import** for **Direction**, two additional fields will appear. **Number of Records** allows us to define how many records will be processed at a time, whereas, **Decimal Separator** defines what separates the fields in the file that is being used to import products.

For example:

Sample data row: `store,manufacturer,`and `price`

Decimal Separator is the comma (,) being used to separate data.

Store

This option allows us to filter the profile to a specific store in our Magento setup. Store-specific fields will be loaded and only this data will be interacted with. It will automatically use this store ID for any data being imported, so that there is no need to declare it in our file when importing. It has the following option: **Default (Admin) Store** - <list of all stores in your Magento setup>.

Selecting **Default (Admin) Store** defines this as a global profile that applies to all stores, so the `store` field in our data will need to be set when importing to specific stores.

File information

File Information consists of the following components, shown below:

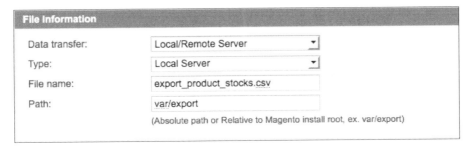

Data transfer

Options: **Interactive** and **Local/Remote Server**.

Interactive (available only for imports), allows us to upload files to be run through the **Run Profile** tab.

Local/Remote Server enables us to fill out the fields to get the file from a source.

Type

Options: **Local Server** and **Remote Server**.

Local Server: The file is located on the same server as our Magento installation or within Magento installation's directories.

Remote Server: We need to connect to an FTP connection to either fetch our file for importing or to store our file after exporting. This will then save the exported file on another server, ready to be used by another system. Else, it will be fetched from an external server and then imported.

 When we select **Remote Server** , we will be asked to insert our FTP information for the connection. This must be filled in for the **Remote Server** connection to work.

Path

Path is the relative path to the file that we use for the profile, minus the trailing slash. It should always be /var/import_folder, rather than /var/import_folder/. There is no need to put our entire root address into the import directory here, just the part after the Magento root directory. If we have it installed in /root/address/magento/, then our path will always be automatically prefixed with this by Magento.

File

File name is the name of the file once in this directory, with file extension, for example: sample.csv.

When using **Remote Server** as our **File Information** type, we must be sure to put our path as relative to the start directory of the FTP connection, once connected. We must always include our directory name in the public HTML folder.

Data Format

Data Format consists of the following components, shown below:

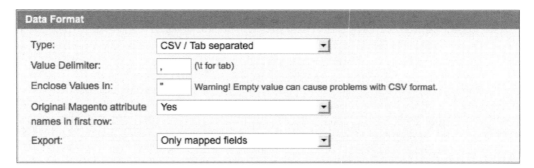

Type

Options: **MS Excel XML** and **CSV/Tab Separated**. This allows us to choose the file type that is going in or out of the profile.

Original Magento attribute names in first row

Options: **Yes** and **No**.

This allows us to define whether or not Magento should check the field names against those that are in the Magento attribute database, when importing. It defines whether we use only field mapping or use it in combination with standard attribute names from the Magneto database. If set to **Yes**, it will match against Magneto attribute names, before looking to the field mapping for answers (about which field to map the value against).

Export

Options: **All fields** and **Only mapped fields**. This is an export only field.

This decides whether our Export profile will export all fields from the Magento attribute database or it will export only the mapping fields that we outline under the **Field Mapping** section.

Field Mapping

Field mapping allows us to control the fields that are imported/exported. It is required before anything is exported, when the **Export** setting under **Data Format** is set to **Only mapped fields**. It is required for fields that don't match their existing names, on importing.

It also allows us to change the labels that fields are exported or imported as. For example, we can export qty as quantity because it's more readable in Excel, or we could change it to output as product_quantity because this file is to be used to import data directly into the database.

Export Filters

This section is extremely valuable when filtering down large datasets for more efficient export profiles. It allows us to put in filters to be applied to our dataset, so that we create profiles that are specific to certain needs. Below, we see the **Export Filters** screen, when exporting products:

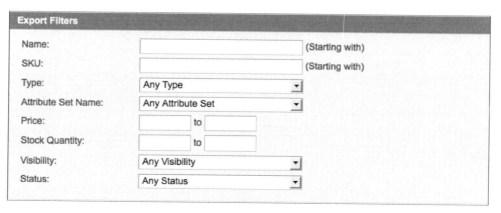

 The **Export Filters** screen only appears when we select **Export** in the **Direction** field.

For example:

- With products, exporting a stock quantity between 0 and 20 would allow us to export those products that are low in stock.

- With products, selecting a certain product type from the **Type** field would allow us to distribute product type management to a relevant department.

- With customers, selecting our wholesale group would allow us to only export our wholesale customers.

- With customers, we can filter by country to get customers from certain countries.

Upload Files

The **Upload Files** tab only appears on import, but allows us to upload files onto the server to be processed. Once we've selected our file, we click **Save and Continue Editing**; this will upload the file onto the server. Once it's uploaded, we select **Run Profile**.

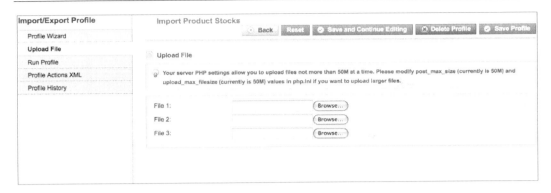

 Upload Files appears only in **Import** profiles and does not relate to **Export** profiles.

Run Profile

This is the section from which we can run our profile. We click on **Run Profile in Popup** to initiate the profile, ensuring beforehand that any changes performed have been saved. Once we have done this, we will be presented with a series of messages until the profile is complete. This will finish with a log of the actions that the script has gone through and some debug messages that keep us posted about the happenings.

If we import, then we will need to upload our files through the **Upload File** tab and select the file from a dropdown before clicking **Run Profile in Popup**.

The profile will not run unless our changes are saved. Hence, we'll need to save changes prior to uploading a file through the profile.

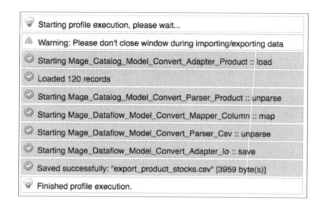

Profile Action XML

From here, we can get the **Profile Action XML** to be placed into the **Advanced Profiles** section within the **Import/Export** menu. This section is advancing our profile beyond what the default profile builder will allow us to do.

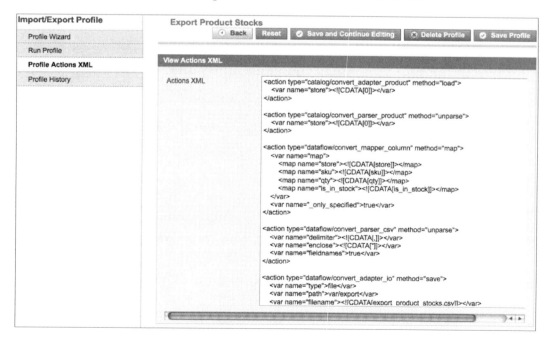

Profile History

This tab has a history of when the current profile was created, updated, and executed. It also provides us with the details of the person who performed these actions.

Sample implementation: Import/Export of metadata

A sample usage of importing/exporting data in Magento is to use it to control the product metadata stored for all of our products. Sometimes SEO (Search Engine Optimization) companies want to tweak metadata en masse. When using Magento's import/export functionality, this reduces the overhead of appointing someone to traverse the data, product-by-product, to edit everything.

To do this, we create:

- An export profile to get all of our product metadata out for us to edit and manage
- An import profile to import all of our changes back into the system

Exporting our metadata

We begin by creating a new profile. For that, we click on the **Add New Profile** button in the top-right of the initial **Profiles** screen.

For setting up our metadata export profile, we have the following settings:

Setting up the Profile Information

This will be a products export profile across all stores and should be named **Export META Data**.

Field	Value
Name	Export META Data
Entity Type	Products
Direction	Export
Store	Default (Admin) Values

Adding the File Information

Our file should be stored in /var/export and be named as meta_data_export.xml on our local server, once the profile has been executed.

Field	Value
Data transfer	Local/Remote server
Type	Local server
File Name	meta_data_export.xml
Path	var/export

Selecting the Data Format

We try an MS Excel XML formatted file with a spreadsheet named Meta Data. This format has its advantages over CSV, as its less prone to formatting issues causing rows to not import. There is more of an internal file structure separating data, which leads to better results when using it.

We set it only to mapped fields which we outline and ensure that Magento attribute names will not be used.

Field	Value
Type	MS Excel XML
Spreadsheet Name	Meta Data
Original Magento Attribute Names	No
in the first row	
Export	Only mapped fields

Mapping our fields

We stick to only meta information fields and the **store/sku** values, so that we have product relation covered when we import back into Magento. To make things a little more interesting, we customize the field names.

Original field	Mapped to
store	store_code
sku	product_sku
meta_title	meta_data_title
meta_keyword	meta_data_keyword
meta_description	meta_data_description

Choosing the Export Filters

Here we limit the number of export filters, so that only enabled products are exported, to cut down on unnecessary changes to products not on the site.

Field	Value
Status	Enabled

Once saved, we go back to the **Run Profile** section to export our file. After this is done, we go into the /var/export directory within the Magento setup directory to find the exported file of product metadata.

When we open this file in MS Excel, it appears nicely (as any normal spreadsheet would), with our spreadsheet name as outlined previously. We make a few random edits, and take note of the products that we have edited for future use, when we wish to ensure that the import has worked.

Importing our metadata

Now that we have our export profile and we've edited all of our data, we need to be able to import our changes back and have Magento process them. To do this, we need to set up a profile to import and process this data correctly.

Now, we set up another profile with the following settings for our import profile:

Setting up the Profile Information

This will be a products import profile across all stores and be named **Import META Data**.

Field	Value
Name	Import META Data
Entity Type	Products
Direction	Import
Store	Default (Admin) Values
Number of records	1
Decimal Separator	.

Adding the File Information

We make the profile interactive, so that we can upload our own file to be executed and processed.

Field	Value
Data transfer	Interactive

Selecting the Data Format

We use MS Excel XML with a spreadsheet named Meta Data, limiting it to only mapped fields (outlined by us). We ensure that Magento attribute names will be used in the first row.

Field	Value
Type	MS Excel XML
Spreadsheet Name	Meta Data
Original Magento Attributes Names	No
in the first row	

Mapping our fields

We map the fields similar to how we did before.

Original field	Mapped to
store	store_code
sku	product_sku
meta_title	meta_data_title
meta_keyword	meta_data_keyword
meta_description	meta_data_description

Once we set this up, we click the **Save and Continue Editing** button and go to **Upload File** on the left sub-navigation menu and upload our changed file via the **Upload File** tab. Then we click on **Save and Continue Editing** and return to the **Run Profile** tab. Then we select the file that we just uploaded from the drop-down list and run our import profile through. The following screenshot will be displayed:

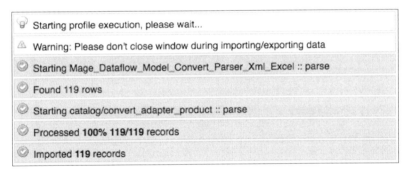

The profile has been imported successfully and the test run updated all the profiles without fail. We check our products via the sku values that we changed under **Manage->Manage Products**. We find that the META data information has now been updated.

Common issues with importing/exporting

The following issues are encountered while importing/exporting.

Bad CSV file formatting

Often the cause of a bad import and missing rows from the import, is that of bad file formatting. This case is more likely to occur in the CSV file format than MS Excel. This happens because the CSV file type is much more prone to data breakages through bad formatting.

Short descriptions

Although we can make sure a short description goes on for as long as we like within Magento, via **Profiles** we should ensure that it isn't more than 255 characters.

Import/export paths

We need to verify that they are writeable. It sounds like an obvious mistake, but many developers don't look at the basics before they look into why everything is going wrong.

Images location

We need to ensure that if we import images with your products, they are placed in `/media/import`. Otherwise, they will throw errors and will not be imported. If the value of our image column is `/sub-directory/image_name.jpg`, then the URL to where the image should be placed within Magento installation is: `media/import/sub-directory/image_name.jpg`.

Importing multiple images

In our CSV/MS Excel XML file, adding either multiple image or small images, or thumb columns to add multiple images into the product, causes a problem.

Summary

In this chapter, we have learned:

- What types of data we can export from Magento from a default installation
- What types of data we can import into Magento from a default installation
- The file types that we can use for these actions
- How to set up our own data profile in order to import/export data ourselves
- How to manage META data en masse using these profiles
- How to solve some of the common issues in the profile functionality

Further to this, we should try and experiment with Magento's import/export data functionality. We should be able to comfortably manage the data profiles that are included in the default Magento installation and should be able to create our own basic profiles.

Index

Thank you for buying
Magento 1.3: PHP Developer's Guide

Packt Open Source Project Royalties

When we sell a book written on an Open Source project, we pay a royalty directly to that project. Therefore by purchasing Magento 1.3: PHP Developer's Guide, Packt will have given some of the money received to the Magento project.

In the long term, we see ourselves and you—customers and readers of our books—as part of the Open Source ecosystem, providing sustainable revenue for the projects we publish on. Our aim at Packt is to establish publishing royalties as an essential part of the service and support a business model that sustains Open Source.

If you're working with an Open Source project that you would like us to publish on, and subsequently pay royalties to, please get in touch with us.

Writing for Packt

We welcome all inquiries from people who are interested in authoring. Book proposals should be sent to author@packtpub.com. If your book idea is still at an early stage and you would like to discuss it first before writing a formal book proposal, contact us; one of our commissioning editors will get in touch with you.

We're not just looking for published authors; if you have strong technical skills but no writing experience, our experienced editors can help you develop a writing career, or simply get some additional reward for your expertise.

About Packt Publishing

Packt, pronounced 'packed', published its first book "Mastering phpMyAdmin for Effective MySQL Management" in April 2004 and subsequently continued to specialize in publishing highly focused books on specific technologies and solutions.

Our books and publications share the experiences of your fellow IT professionals in adapting and customizing today's systems, applications, and frameworks. Our solution-based books give you the knowledge and power to customize the software and technologies you're using to get the job done. Packt books are more specific and less general than the IT books you have seen in the past. Our unique business model allows us to bring you more focused information, giving you more of what you need to know, and less of what you don't.

Packt is a modern, yet unique publishing company, which focuses on producing quality, cutting-edge books for communities of developers, administrators, and newbies alike. For more information, please visit our website: www.PacktPub.com.

Magento 1.3 Theme Design

ISBN: 978-1-847196-64-4   Paperback: 188 pages

Customize the appearance of your Magento
e-commerce store with Magento's powerful theming
engine

1. Give your Magento stores a unique branded
    look and feel by creating your own Magento
    themes

2. Use design techniques to reinforce your brand
    message and increase sales

3. Customise your Magento theme's look, feel,
    layout, and features

Magento: Beginner's Guide

ISBN: 978-1-847195-94-4   Paperback: 300 pages

Create a dynamic, fully featured, online store with the
most powerful open source e-commerce software

1. Step-by-step guide to building your own online
    store

2. Focuses on the key features of Magento that
    you must know to get your store up and
    running

3. Customize the store's appearance to make it
    uniquely yours

4. Clearly illustrated with screenshots and a
    working example

Please check **www.PacktPub.com** for information on our titles

1529849R0

Printed in Great Britain by
Amazon.co.uk, Ltd.,
Marston Gate.